THRIFT
SHOP
DECORATING

THRIFT SHOP DECORATING

by ADELE WILLIAMS

ARBOR HOUSE

NEW YORK

THRIFT
SHOP
DECORATING

§§

INTRODUCTION

§§

DO you ever leaf through the pages of the glossy decorating magazines and turn away in frustration because the rooms shown could not possibly be duplicated for less than several thousand dollars? Then this book is for you, because my theory is that a pretty house or apartment need not cost a pretty penny.

What it takes to make over your house precisely to your taste is a little (but not much) work, a lot of imagination and the courage to get rid of preconceived ideas of what is necessary and what is not. An attractive place to live requires that three basic principles be put to work: An orderly symmetrical arrangement of rooms and furniture, appropriate color and freshness, and finally the wit of the unexpected accent to give life and spark to the room. The first costs nothing at all, the second and third require more taste and know-how than cash.

Accept the principle that "less is more," that an uncluttered, clean room given the benefit of a logical and pleasant arrangement of furniture can be attractive for pennies.

This is not to say you don't need money at all. But if you realize what you are after is comfort and elegant simplicity, you are well on your way.

I recently worked with a client on her country cottage, which she wanted to rent for needed income. At first glance it seemed hopeless; she had practically no money to spend, yet no one in his or her right mind would pay the fairly substantial rent she was asking. Her basic plan was to rent the cottage for the summer season for enough money to make yearly mortgage payments.

The house itself was charming, an old saltbox with a center chimney and four working fireplaces, but it was choking to death with clutter and inappropriate furniture. The first job was to create some breathing space. We removed the huge white shag rug that dwarfed the living room. Next, an enormous mirrored coffee table and an elaborate, gilt-framed—but sleazy-looking—mirror were sent to the local resale shop to raise a bit of cash. After much discussion my client was talked out of a fabric featuring huge animals that she had chosen (and wanted to have quilted) to cover the simple sofa and two comfortable chairs. Finally she agreed to substitute plain blue denim at a fraction of the cost. An old, pretty French backgammon table, which had been hidden behind the barn was placed between two windows and flanked by a pair of simple Queen-Anne-style dining chairs (circa 1920 and purchased at the local thrift shop for three dollars apiece) which were antiqued a dark blue. Since the walls were paneled and the floor good-looking old random-width oak, we simply waxed both to a soft gleam. For a coffee table we painted an old captain's trunk (seven dollars at the local Army/Navy store) a deep, dark red and added a pair of blue Canton plates as ashtrays, plus a couple of pots of ivy. Plain organdy tie-back curtains gave just the right look. The major project for the mantelpiece was to get rid of the miscellaneous clutter and leave only a handsome pair of brass candle holders. Our single extravagance was an antique brass coal scuttle, which we filled with marvelous paper—not plastic—zinnias.

We went through the whole house the same way. None of the rooms was as bad as the living room, but simply by removing faded, elaborate bedspreads and substituting fresh checked gingham or piqué blanket covers, rolling up worn, elaborate rugs and replacing fussy, faded lamp shades with crisp, pleated white paper ones, we made the little house come alive. The happy ending: this client rented her house to a charming couple the very first weekend it was advertised—for even more money than she had hoped, and she had the enormous satisfaction of meeting the mortgage payments and saving her charming little house for herself.

What made Ellen and her house happy may not sound like your style, maybe you hate organdy curtains and despise blue; the country-cottage look may be just what you don't want. But that is not my point here. Whether your taste runs to sleek modern done in neutral tones, or to the traditional look of luxury, the principle remains the same. Clear out what doesn't fit, build your room around the colors you like, arrange your furniture so that it lives well, and you'll be happy with your house. It can be done at thrift-shop prices. This is not empty advice. I've done it over and over again—ugly little apartments, charming town houses, vacation cottages, grand houses that were left to people who no longer had grand incomes—you name it and I've done it over these past twenty-five years. And I've had fun accepting the challenge of making dreary quarters into comfortable "living" space. You can do it, too. In these pages I've outlined all the tricks I have learned, borrowed or stolen from topflight decorators. Put them to work for yourself—you'll enjoy every minute of it.

§§

CHAPTER ONE

THE HONEST
DECORATOR

§§

IN writing this book I have tried to include all the things that really count. It would be a simple task to pad it with meaningless advice on how to mix your own paint, design a floor plan, paint a wall, and so forth. I hope I will be able to give you something more valuable than that. I cannot tell you how to place your furniture; I don't know what your particular room is like. But I can give you some valuable guidelines on what will work and what will not.

To begin at the beginning . . . If you have a front yard or garden, it is essential that it be neat and inviting—free of miscellaneous hardware, children's toys and other clutter. It takes little effort and practically no money to have a walkway bordered by flowering plants, and all you need to spend to keep a garden invitingly neat is about an hour a week with a rake and/or lawn mower.

But whether your front door is marked as anonymously as "4C" or blooms at the end of a charming path, you can make it distinctive. Paint it if possible (most landlords will give permission, and if it's your own house, who's to stop you?). I like a front door painted dark shiny green or red, or even lemon-peel yellow, and marked with a brilliant knocker. No cash to pay for a large brass door knocker? . . . Think nothing of it—stop in any variety store and buy a big shiny metal or plastic towel ring. Towel rings serve amazingly well as door knockers—and cost only a couple of dollars. Now choose some sort of dramatic-looking tree or plant (if there is light near your door) set out in a big tub. Again, this doesn't have to cost a lot. A small, bushy pine tree dug up free in the woods—or purchased at little cost from a roadside nursery—can be planted in a small washtub that you have first enameled glossy black. (Don't forget to punch a few holes in the bottom first, to assure drainage.)

Now into the house, or apartment. You have a hallway or entranceway? Lucky you! If so, don't overcrowd it with furniture, even if you have money to burn. Since hallways and/or entrance foyers are usually small, I always paint them a light color to create an illusion of space. The color should relate to the living-room walls, but surprisingly enough yellow often turns out to be a wonderful entranceway color. Yellow is cheerful, space-enlarging, and never seems to "fight" with other colors. Mirrors, the great space creators, are especially effective in hallways. A generous-sized mirror (see living room chapter for how to obtain one at little cost) can add greatly to space and represents a lot of decoration at the same time. As for entranceway furniture, a small narrow table that will hold a lamp, plus a pair of side chairs, will suffice. Both are usually available at thrift shops, and they look great if antiqued dark red or moss green. As for a rug: halls take a beating from the elements, so I like to use straw matting, which is both attractive and practical as well as inexpensive to replace. Vinyl is also a good choice if you can afford it.

Now we are in the house and—since living and dining rooms, bedrooms and baths, as well as kitchens, are important enough to be given chapters of their own—I'd like to go on to some general principles of decorating that I hope you will find useful in building the environment you will enjoy living in.

First of all, there is nothing mysterious or tricky about decorating. Your objective is to create a comfortable, pleasing room, and the elements are simple. Let's take floor plans, for example. Forget about those little boxes that are supposed to show you how to arrange furniture. There is only one way to arrange furniture and that is by pushing it around until you find the arrangement that is the most comfortable and attractive for *you*. Now, if this sounds overly simple, stop and think for a minute. In living rooms, the sofa should be at right angles to either a fireplace or a substantial table that is centered on the longest wall; or you can center the sofa itself against the longest wall. Where should the coffee table go? Naturally it is going to be used by whoever is sitting on the sofa, so the coffee table has to be in front of the sofa. There should be chairs drawn up to the coffee table because people in the room are going to want to talk to people sitting on the sofa. Since there has to be light in the room, tables will have to hold lamps near enough to be useful to the people sitting in the chairs and on the sofa. Logical?

You must concern yourself with "balancing" the room. If a heavy group, such as a sofa and chairs, is going to be on one side of the room, naturally you are going to want something of weight and interest on the opposite wall: that something could be anything from a group of windows facing out onto a terrace or garden to a grand piano. Only you will be able to decide —because it is your room. The way to arrange furniture is to keep moving things around until you come up with a "balance" that pleases you. The same holds true for any room. In a bedroom the largest piece of furniture is the bed or beds, so you probably want to put the next largest piece, usually a chest of drawers, on the opposite wall. Furniture placement *happens* with an amazing ease and logic.

The same logical approach holds true for color. Nobody works from those old-fashioned color wheels—the kind that are supposed to show you what colors complement each other- —anymore. If you are confused about color, look around you. Nature's color schemes always work. Later in this book (page 30) I describe several natural color schemes. If you stick to clear natural colors, you won't make a mistake. Pick the colors you like and put them together the way nature does. You love blue? Then remember how a clear blue sky "goes with" all the varied greens of trees and plants, the brown and gray of tree bark, the beige and tans of shells or sand on the beach. Forget about trying to match or contrast colors. No good decorator does. The only colors that are hard to work with are the harsh, artificial ones, like magenta or bright, hard orange—colors that rarely occur in nature.

Some people like to talk about monochromatic or contrasting color schemes. I think this is pretentious rot. The really splendid houses of the world never have "color schemes," simply a blend of soft, pretty colors. If you want to understand how to mix colors, spend as much time as you can afford studying illustrated books on great houses; observe how beautiful houses are never "color co-ordinated"—they are simply a mélange of lovely things, each one beautiful in itself. One book I particularly recommend is *Vogue's Book of Houses, Gardens and People* (Condé Nast Press, New York). Invest in it if possible. The rooms shown are the best of the best.

Learn to train your eye to recognize beauty—in a sea shell, in a piece of fruit or a vegetable. Is there anything more handsome than a fresh eggplant? . . . the soft olive green of the leaves, the shimmering glow of its deep purple skin, a true color scheme. There is harmony and beauty in a Japanese white-paper fan, to be purchased for a dollar or two . . . or in a Coromandel screen worth thousands.

To give another example: a pot of inexpensive ivy is charming in a real clay pot; it is obscene in a plastic one. Why? Because if you look (and few people really do), the terra cotta pot has texture and color that are soft and pleasing to the eye. And the clay pot is real earth, not an imitation; the plastic is inappropriate and phony.

Real, natural textures, such as wood, brick, stone, silk, cotton and linen, are unfailingly lovely; they are timeless and their beauty endures. They are never offensive. It is only when we substitute the artificial for the genuine that we are heading for trouble. I realize that we live in a plastic age, and I accept the convenience plastic has brought us. But in decorating our houses for enduring pleasure, we must look for the real and natural colors and textures that no man-made substitute can ever approach.

What color expert can match the harmony of a farm basket of fresh eggs? The warm honey hue of the basket, the creamy white and brown of the eggs. You might easily build a charming room around just this combination. It is only when we fall prey to the garish, the pretentious, the fake, that we make mistakes in decorating, in dress, in food—in fact, in life.

What has all this to do with thrift shop decorating? Simply this: you can create beautiful, inviting rooms for little money when you forget what I call the "color scheme syndrome." You will then see the beauty in faded English chintz curtains piled on a dusty shelf in a thrift shop—as I once did, and was rewarded with the loveliest curtains I ever owned, right down to the flannel interlining, of a quality I could never have afforded new. These were curtains that drew cozily across my windows night after night, year after year. And I never stopped to think if they would "go with" my other furnishings. They were beautiful and could only give pleasure. I once found a remnant of real silk, not part of any color scheme, that I promptly bought to cover a chair seat. No, it did not "go" with anything; it was simply lovely on its own and could contribute only beauty. Learning to decorate like this, by training your eye, allows you to substitute a wonderful old basket found for three dollars for a pretentious decorative piece. It allows you to see that a gleaming bare wood floor is to be infinitely preferred to yards of synthetic, garish carpeting; to know that a glowing fire can do as much for a room as a Rembrandt, and that a simple sofa covered in cotton duck at two dollars a yard is far more elegant than imitation silk or nylon velvet.

No matter how much or how little you spend, the success of your rooms depends almost entirely on cultivating your eye for beauty. The best decorating advice I can give you is to look—in museums, at books, in elegant shops, at other people's houses; study fine and beautiful things even if you have no way of affording them. When you recognize beauty, you will find it at your own price; when you begin to realize how much more

Boston rocker.

effective a basket is for flowers—compared to a more elaborate container—you have indeed trained your eye. And decorating becomes a pleasurable hobby, not a nerve-racking chore. If I can offer any really sound decorating advice, it is contained in a one-word sentence: *Look*. Don't tolerate ugliness. Throw out anything that displeases you; insist on beauty around you, and you will have it, always.

As for the practical, mundane, but necessary, "how to" . . . well, help is at hand. There's no longer any need for the messy job of mixing your own paint to get the color you want. Modern paint stores located in every town in the United States have hundreds of color "chips" to choose from, and an employee will mix your paint by machine to assure an even, smooth finish. Furthermore, he will help you select the right type of paint for the job and—if you are going to do it yourself—will sell you the exact equipment you will need.

It is no longer necessary to approach the making of a table skirt or a pair of curtains with fear and trembling. Basic patterns for these and other decorative accents (such as pillows) are sold from coast to coast. There is even a special tape that will pinch-pleat your curtains for you.

What is most interesting about decorating today is that there are no set rules or limits. Gone are the days when one would not dare to mix two or three different patterns or prints in one room. Gone too are the outworn clichés about "children's colors" or "men's colors." I feel that an infant's room should be decorated to please the eye of mama and papa. I even did one baby's room in black and white checked gingham. The furniture (secondhand, of course) was sprayed white, and the accent piece was a black Boston rocker with a big red cushion. A tray of red geraniums sat in a sunny window. The mother of the baby was intensely pleased with the effect.

I once had a man tell me: "You know, I really like pink." Well, why not? We painted the walls of his bedroom a good strong geranium pink, the blanket covers, cushions and curtains were of brown and black plaid, and the furniture was painted shiny black. We added cushions of still another pink. The room was a success.

My point: relax and enjoy decorating; train your eye for beauty, and you will find it at a price you can afford to pay.

§§§

CHAPTER TWO

WHAT YOU NEED IS A DUMP TRUCK

§§§

UNLESS you are starting from absolute scratch (and that we will take up in the next chapter), your first step toward creating the house you want is to get rid of what you don't like, as well as the unnecessary. If it is awful-looking, worn beyond repair, or you simply hate it, get it out of your house!

This goes for everything that does not contribute to clean and uncluttered living—the odd bits of china and glass that you've been meaning to throw out, the worn and useless cooking utensils, that awful plastic table in the kitchen, Aunt Minnie's chipped cut-glass vase, the rug that doesn't fit and looks dingy besides, and the meaningless clutter of ornaments, souvenirs, and photos of people you don't even like. Get all of it out of your living space and your life. "But," you may protest, "I have to have a kitchen table and I can't get rid of all the rugs, the place will look like a barn." It might, momentarily, but the ugly plastic table can be replaced by a secondhand garden table from almost any thrift shop for under fifteen dollars. Give it a fresh coat of paint, and you'll feel happier every time you sit down to have your morning coffee. The price you can get for some of the ugly things you don't like (but someone else needs) can go toward something you will really enjoy.

If there are some things you simply can't bear to part with, but you know they are messing up your house, pack them up and store them in the basement or attic. You can always review them periodically for later use if you must.

The important thing is to clear the decks, get down to the essentials, and then start your own decorating plan. I'm assuming this means you will be left with at least a sofa, a couple of chairs and a table or two in the living room, a dining table and chairs, and basic bedroom furniture.

The next step is to decide what colors you like to live with, and this depends on the kind of person you are. Do you like a fresh, open-air atmosphere with lots of sunlight and fresh-flower colors? Or do you prefer the calm, collected beiges and browns of wheat, sand and stones? Or perhaps you want your rooms to envelop you with a cozy warmth of deep, dark colors (I call them London colors) that close out the outside world?

Let's try on a few color schemes for size. Assuming you are the flower-garden type, your walls could be painted a clear sky blue, the furniture upholstered in a pale lilac sailcloth. And before I go a step further: Thrift Shop Decorating Rule Number One is *no wallpaper*—it is expensive and difficult to apply; the good patterns are astronomical in price, and you can get endlessly tired of the pattern long before the paper is worn out. The same goes for printed slipcover fabrics: good prints are usually much more expensive than solid colors, and once on the furniture, you are locked into a look that cannot be changed without a large outlay of cash. If you find a print you feel you cannot live without, buy a small piece and make some pillows for your sofa; the expense is negligible and the effect is big.

Now where are we? We have blue-sky walls, lilac slipcovers and, let's hope, a white ceiling; but the printed fabric you've found that you *must* have has neither lilac nor blue in it. It is, perhaps, all yellow and pink with a touch of red or orange, or whatever. Go ahead, try to think how nature combines color. Picture a beautiful English garden under a blue summer sky; the flowers run the gamut of the spectrum and they all "go together" beautifully. I'm always sorry for the people I see frantically running around with a bit of carpet in one hand and a swatch of fabric in the other, anxiously trying to match the exact shade of green or blue. It's all so unnecessary and makes for an endlessly dull room. I once saw a room in a well-known New York store done entirely in green and white, right down to a magazine with a green-and-white cover on the coffee table . . . What do you do when a new issue comes out—relocate?

Now what can we put on the floor of our "garden" room? A green rug? Fine. A small oriental in faded colors? A needle-point floral that you perhaps made yourself? All good choices. But here is Thrift Shop Decorating Rule Number Two: *no wall-to-wall carpet*. It's expensive, difficult to clean, and you are going to tire of it long before you recover from the shock of paying the price. If you really want to save money, buy an appropriate-sized carpet remnant (it doesn't have to be huge; don't be afraid of bare floors, they give a room character), then have heavy carpet fringe sewn all around it. The result is quite elegant and expensive-looking.

But perhaps flower colors turn you off; you love the serenity of neutrals. There's no doubt about it; pale beige and tan and straw colors have a clean, calm look that lives well—especially if you are the kind of person who likes lots of books and magazines lying around, even a work table with a typewriter and the usual clutter of desk paraphernalia. I once did a studio apartment for an author (a struggling one) that worked well for him. He had a rather nice old sofa with good simple lines and a couple of comfortable chairs plus a studio bed. We threw out a motley collection of broken-down "mahogany" end tables and a ghastly rug that had been ugly when it was new. Then, to give a look of spaciousness, we covered the scratched, unfinished floors with straw matting. Straw matting is very inexpensive if you buy it in squares and put it down yourself. It is also wonderfully easy to keep clean—just vacuum, and if something spills on one of the squares, pick the square up and wash it. The walls were painted the color of natural bamboo, and the sofa and chairs were covered in white sailcloth—yes, here I go again with sailcloth, but it's cheap, durable and effective. (Write to Lowenstein and Sons, 111 West 40th Street, New York, N.Y. 10018, for a source near you. They make an excellent quality sailcloth.) We made a fitted cover of brown velveteen for the studio bed and covered two square bolsters with the same brown to take away the curse of the "bed look." A Parsons table purchased at the unfinished furniture store was enameled black and the author's collection of shells was arranged on it. A simple shelf wide enough for four people to dine comfortably, or to serve as a buffet table, was built along one wall and again enameled black. On it, an old rush basket of dried wheat. The only real treasure my client had was an antique Chinese ginger jar in deep blue that had been made into a lamp. It was just what the room needed to lift it out of the too-matched look. The simple background made his welter of writing materials, books and papers seem not clutter at all but part of a room that lived extremely well.

All this may sound fine, but what you want is a cozy, luxurious hideaway where you can close out the world—a room that shuts out the gloom of night and welcomes you to your own private place. Truman Capote, that master of words, described his apartment, which had crimson red walls, as being like a hot raspberry tart (and I can imagine it was).

If this is the feeling you want, start as always by getting rid of what you don't want and can't use. Be ruthless, especially about tacky little ornaments and small tipsy tables. Once you've arrived at the survival scene and are wondering what on earth you are going to do with all this bare space, get some color on the walls; it will do wonders to "furnish" the room instantly. For this type of room I like to go to a dark color, deep olive green, plum, a warm brown or—if you are daring—a deep crimson. My favorite is olive green—just be sure it's dark enough. It simply never fails, every color looks marvelous with it and most people never tire of it. Let's say you decide on the olive walls, then the furniture has to be covered. For this type of room I'll forgo my beloved sailcloth in favor of glazed chintz: it has a nice silky, luxurious quality but is still inexpensive and practical. My first color choice would be a deep plum. Here again is nature's combination of colors—the dark olive green of grape leaves and the lustrous sheen of purple grapes or plums. Curtains of course in the same shade, lined in pale blue and hung on traverse rods so they can be drawn across at night. But nothing elaborate, just straight "make them yourself " panels sewn with self-pleating tape that comes by the yard in all good drapery departments. The spark of color for this type of room might be a half dozen or so silk pillows for the sofa, all in different colors. Sounds expensive? Not at all; Siamese silk can be ordered for about six dollars a yard, one-half yard will make a fourteen-inch square pillow. (You can write to Far Eastern Fabrics, 171 Madison Avenue, New York, N.Y. 10016, for fabrics.) Incidentally, unless you have money to burn, don't bother with down pillows. The new polyester fill is just as soft, much cleaner and one-tenth the price. You can make your own pillows in muslin; stuff them with polyester and then make the covers with a simple cording finish—for less than five dollars each.

What to put on the floor? Well, an Oriental rug, a real one, not the awful machine-made ones, is the perfect answer. Orientals are expensive, but if you are willing to accept a slightly tattered one (I like them thin and worn myself) a small one can usually be found at an Oriental rug dealer's, or can be picked up at an auction. Don't be embarrassed to ask if they have something too worn to be on display—I've made some very good buys that way.

Obviously any room has to have some tables, and I've found that the "world traveler" look can take rattan stools that usually come three to a set. They serve nicely as coffee or end tables. Finally, you'll need some sort of oblong table that can serve for buffets or be set up as a bar on one end, with a lamp on the other. If you look, you can often find old library tables, carved and intricate and in a way so ugly they have the heavy character that adds just the right "anchorage." If not, I always rely on the unpainted Parsons table; this time I'd paint it a dark antique red. A pair of dining-table chairs almost always available in thrift shops could be painted to match. Look for the Queen Anne style with curved legs, and be sure they have what are known as slip seats. This means the seats unscrew and slip out

Library table.

and can easily be recovered with a staple gun and the leftover fabric from the slip covers.

So much for a few pointers on what you can do if you have something to start with. Later on we'll get down to specific problems like lighting, accessories, curtains or no curtains, floor coverings and finishes, bedrooms, bathrooms and kitchens.

§§

CHAPTER THREE

STARTING FROM SCRATCH

§§

I once moved into an apartment with nothing but a single box spring, a mattress, and a borrowed lamp. Furthermore, I was extremely broke. But the apartment I found was a dream for the price: a hundred dollars a month for a medium-size studio, with sleeping alcove, spacious bathroom, tiny kitchen, and a mammoth terrace. A real *find*.

I immediately imagined the possibilities for this empty room. But where to start?

If you must begin with no furniture and very little cash, the first purchase should be a sofa. This is the anchor piece that will contribute more to your room than any other. Now the best way to get the best sofa for the least money is to start canvassing the small upholstery shops in your area. Ask if they have any unclaimed sofas or if they have an old one they would like to

Lawson sofa.

rebuild for you. The first is more desirable—you know exactly what you are getting. Unclaimed sofas are usually cheaper because the upholsterer is stuck with his work and will often be willing to sell for just enough to cover his expense. These shops often have great chairs, too: but don't be in a hurry to buy upholstered chairs if money is a problem. There are other ways to solve seating arrangements that cost far less than upholstered chairs, and I'll discuss chairs in a later chapter. Do, however, keep your eye out for an upholstered bench, even if it is in tattered condition. An upholstered bench is easily recovered with a small piece of fabric, neatly mitered at the corners, and the raw edges hidden with braid held on by decorative brass tacks. A bench gives lots of seating as well as decoration for the money.

If you possibly can, buy your sofa covered in muslin; this way you are not locked into some ghastly print that will show through slipcover fabric. Don't let the upholsterer talk you into a more expensive piece because he tells you "the fabric alone is worth the price"—you don't want the fabric at any price. Now we come to the Thrift Shop Decorating Rule Number Three: *Never recover furniture with upholstery.* Once it is on, it is impossible to clean and it locks you into a color scheme you may grow to hate. Buy furniture in muslin and make, or have made, slipcovers. Some of the most elegant rooms in America have slipcovers on every upholstered piece. They can be as luxurious as you can afford. I've seen pieces in one of the DuPont mansions slipcovered in silk brocade at $125 a yard. Why? Because the covers can be removed and carefully cleaned. But here we are talking about lots for little, and slipcovers will give you just that. They can be made of any fairly sturdy material that goes happily into the washing machine. Put the covers back on still slightly damp, and there you are, fresh as paint at practically no cost at all. My own favorites for slipcovers are light-weight sailcloth, which comes in just about any color you want, including my favorite white, striped ticking, denim, and glazed chintz. The last I like to use for a more formal effect.

Failing to find a decent sofa in an upholstery shop, the next best thing is to try the Household Goods for Sale column in the local newspaper. You can often get a good buy. It will probably be covered in something horrible like wine-colored crushed velvet, but sailcloth can come to your rescue; it's opaque enough to cover most upholstery sins. The big thing is not to panic and rush into the nearest furniture store only to spend $1,200 to $1,500 on a possibly inferior sofa at that. Incidentally, the big trick in buying a used rebuilt sofa is to look for simple lines—preferably the classic "Lawson" sofa identified by the three loose seat cushions and three for the back. If you are unfamiliar with the style, check your nearest furniture store. Any classic design is desirable, such as Chippendale, Duncan Phyfe and Sheraton, but these are more difficult to slipcover.

Of course, there are exceptions to every rule. I once bought a lovely old reproduction of a Duncan Phyfe sofa upholstered in olive green velvet for $100. It blended perfectly in the room and the slipcover issue was bypassed completely.

One final note about slipcovers: they must always go to the floor—and box pleats should be avoided at all costs. A neat, simple pleat in each corner is perfect.

If all other efforts fail, you can purchase an extra-narrow box spring and mattress. Ask for the thirty-inch width; everything wider looks too "beddy." Buy rectangular foam rubber bolsters to form the back. Finally, use a tailored slipcover. If this is going to be your plan, then it is wise to deviate from the list of fabrics above and use cotton corduroy or velveteen in a fairly dark color, deep brown, olive green, dark blue, etc. The velveteen has a nice, rich look that does away with the "day-bed" look.

After you know which sofa will be yours, but before you have finalized the slipcover color, you should decide on the color for the walls. If you are really on a tight budget, paint them a dark color; again, my favorites are olive green, a soft brown or plum (not purple). Some people like dark blue walls. I find them depressing. A dark color, however, helps enormously to "furnish" a room. Once the wall color is established, then pick a light color for the sofa, it makes the room look bigger, more furnished. Let's say you decide on soft brown walls; white or very pale blue sailcloth will look great on the sofa.

The exception here is the velveteen-covered box spring and mattress idea—velveteen just doesn't look good in pastel colors, but a deep, creamy beige is fine with brown walls. Or you can use a warm brown with dark green walls. For the plum, try a deep blue.

Sooner or later you are going to have to eat, and will want a comfortable place to do it. This means buying a table and chairs. The cheapest and most attractive way to get around this problem is either to buy or have made the most inexpensive round table top of plywood and have it mounted on a sturdy base of wood or metal or even rigid plastic. The top should be about thirty-nine inches in diameter and about twenty-nine inches from the floor. This is a comfortable height and a good size for four place settings. If you have a separate dining room and a larger family, the top can be made of a forty-eight-inch round plywood to seat six comfortably. The table is then covered to the floor with a round cloth. To look really proper, your table is going to need a flannel liner, but liners are easy to make and need only to have the edges pinked—no hemming necessary. Now, for the cloth itself, here is the place to use a personal-favorite print. It takes only six yards to make a "to the floor" cover for a forty-eight-inch table, if your fabric is forty-eight to fifty inches wide, and frequently (if you can't make it yourself) the labor cost of the local dressmaker is not too high. And, by making more than one, you can change the prints periodically.

Again, light colors will give a more furnished look, but this doesn't mean it has to be floral. If you hate florals, geometrics or animal prints, anything that appeals to your own taste can be used. Try to keep the color scheme related, not matched, simply with some connection to what you are doing. For example, in the room with dark green walls and a blue or white sofa, you could have a mixed floral of any type as long as the colors are the natural ones found in real flowers—not those "strange" prints that show black roses and magenta daisies. These are to be avoided.

If you don't want a floral, a green and white bamboo print or a fern print is pretty. It doesn't have to be an olive green. Nature mixes greens, and so can you.

If you are using the brown-beige scheme, an animal print can be amusing; all sorts of friendly jungle beasts abound in inexpensive fabrics. Or try a print of sunflowers or daisies on a white or yellow ground. One of my favorite prints is geraniums—pink or red—on a white ground. It seems to go with almost anything. Black background prints are enjoying popularity at this writing, but they require light walls and a bigger budget to work into a scheme.

Dining chairs are really the easiest of thrift shop decorating items. For some unknown reason there always seem to be sets of four or six dining room chairs available at very low prices. If you are not so lucky in a standard thrift shop, try the Salvation Army or the local newspapers. Don't be put off by a golden oak or garish red-mahogany finish. If the chairs have fairly decent lines they can look very good antiqued. Do, however, stay with the dark colors. Antique white is not as effective as dark red, olive green or deep blue. Everything depends on the colors of your room and your print, though. Most of all, don't be afraid of dark red; it seems to work with most color plans.

Now that we have a sofa and a place to dine in the living room (or more luxuriously in a separate dining room), the next thought is some seating arrangement that will be comfortable, pleasant and cheap. If I have little money, I usually don't place the sofa against the wall, as this leaves a large area of bare space to be filled in with something—and that something costs money. Try placing your sofa at a right angle to the wall as though you had a fireplace. If you are lucky enough to have a fireplace, it will be the focal point in the room. Not having one, however, doesn't mean that this arrangement won't work. Pull up the bench, mentioned earlier—this time without the cushion—to the sofa and flank it with two chairs. The focal point, in the absence of a fireplace, can be a generous-sized oblong table, a secondhand library table or perhaps an unfinished Parsons table. Paint it a good dark color, for example, black lacquer. Place a sizable lamp on the table. But, please, a plain one; the best for the least is a Chinese ginger-jar shape with a crisp pleated white paper shade.

Now for the chairs; there are loads of choices. For instance, handsome old wing-back chairs can often be found at thrift shops and covered to match the sofa. Failing that, I've often used the unfinished copies of Louis XV French chairs available at the Door Stores. Do you have one in your neighborhood? Mine is at 210 East 51st Street, New York, New York 10022. These chairs are highly effective when stained a deep walnut and given puffy cushions to soften them. If Louis XV is not your cup of tea, try wicker or rattan. A so-called peacock chair —sometimes available secondhand, and not terribly expensive brand new—adds a lot of drama and solid comfort with its high fan back, and can be complemented by the bench. A good source for wicker and rattan furniture, rugs and accessories is Walters Wicker Wonderland, 991 Second Avenue, New York, New York 10021. Whatever you do, don't be talked into those dreary so-called "club chairs" that squat on the floor like fat old ladies.

You are going to want some sort of coffee table and an end table or two. Once again, if money is a real problem, and it always is for me, I like those sets of rattan stools up-ended and equipped with generous-sized unmatched plates as ashtrays. Rattan is both serviceable and good-looking.

Victorian chair.

Remember, what you are after is comfort as well as good looks. The sofa should look inviting with some nice soft cushions, a table at hand for a drink or an ashtray. The chairs should face the sofa so you can sit and talk to your friends and family. There should be a table large enough for at least one big lamp, some magazines, perhaps a tray set up as a simple bar. The colors should be pleasing and relate to natural combinations. There should be a place to dine pleasantly. After that come what I call the extras, curtains, simple ones, just straight to the floor but full enough to pull across at night for a cozy, comfortable feeling. We'll discuss rugs and ornaments in a later chapter, along with details about bedrooms, bathrooms and accessories, but in the meantime the basic mix of good colors, simple furniture and a logical, comfortable arrangement will have you off to a good start.

§§§

CHAPTER FOUR

THE LIVING ROOM

§§§

NOW that we have decided on color schemes and basic furniture for thrift shop decorating, let's get down to specific rooms and their potential. You will be spending much of your time in the living room. It comes first. You will entertain there, and unless you have the luxury of a full dining room, you will no doubt often dine there, too. I think it's incredibly dreary to eat every meal in the kitchen.

Your first step, whether you have something to begin with or are starting from scratch, is your color plan. As I mentioned before, decide which colors give you most pleasure. If you want to be absolutely sure you are going to like your room, stick to combinations of colors found in nature. By this I don't mean a rigid "apple blossom room" of pink, green, and brown, but the true colors of nature—browns, beiges, greens, grays. Off-beat, peculiar colors like magenta or chartreuse are hard to handle, and even harder to live with.

Forget about exposure and that old, worn-out theory that dark northern exposure means the walls must be white or yellow. Personally, I hate white walls. They usually turn yellowish within a few weeks and require endless washing or repainting to keep reasonably fresh. If you like a light shade, use a pastel. The key to the color is the size of the room and how much furniture you want to put into it. If the room is small and you have a lot of furniture to fit in, it's usually best to select a light color, for example, pale blue, creamy apricot, pale lilac, sunshine yellow. Light walls *do* make a room look larger.

If on the other hand you have a big, barnlike room and very little furniture, a dark color, as mentioned before, will go a long way to make it look furnished. (For some suggested colors, see Chapter Two.)

The next step is how to arrange furniture for comfort, convenience and good looks. First, never place a large piece of furniture off-center. In the Introduction I described a summer cottage that a client and I made over with practically no money. In the living room, for some strange reason, the sofa was pushed to one end of the wall opposite the fireplace, where it looked like some poor dog cowering in the corner. Sofas don't have to go against the wall, you know; they can be placed at a right angle to the wall and faced with a pair of chairs, or a chair and bench. You can place this grouping around a fireplace if you are lucky enough to have one, or flanking a good-sized long, narrow table. Look for the old library tables I've mentioned, or an unpainted Parsons table. What is desired is comfort; if you are going to use the long table, a pair of lamps—one at each end—will give each group enough light to read by easily. Coffee tables are not an absolute necessity, but you do need a place for an ashtray, or a drink, or your after-dinner coffee. I like to forgo the usual coffee tables one sees in furniture stores—they are clichéed and expensive. Up-ended wicker stools are handy (I've mentioned these before); the largest of the set can go between two chairs, the other smaller two in front of the sofa.

Of course if your grouping is in front of a fireplace, then some sort of more substantial table is needed. I've found a long, narrow Parsons table in back of the sofa a good answer. These are available unpainted, at low cost, and can be given a coat of shiny enamel for dramatic effect. My favorites are dark red, black or white, all glossy. This table can hold the needed lamp or lamps, with the wicker stools in front of the sofa. Now speaking of chairs, wing chairs add great character and a sub-stantial look. Or you can use the unpainted French chairs discussed in the previous chapter. Still another way is to face your sofa with a small love seat; if this is your choice, balance the "weight" of the sofa by adding a good sized, preferably round, table on the love seat side. The easiest solution to this problem is a skirted table. This, as I have mentioned before, need only be a plywood top on a metal, wood or plastic base; thirty-six inches is a desirable diameter and twenty-nine inches from the floor. Covered with a flannel liner, then a print or solid-color cloth, it can add a great deal of furnished look for little money. If you can afford it, have a glass top made to go over the fabric, but this is not a necessity with the new stain-resistant fabrics. Your table can hold a lamp and a good-sized ashtray. And there you have the beginning of a successful room. A comfortable arrangement where you can sit and talk, listen to the Sunday symphony, or just read and relax.

One very special tip: If your house or apartment doesn't have a hallway, face your sofa away from the front door. Just presenting the back of the sofa gives some definition to a room and creates a sense of privacy that is a great comfort.

I know I have mentioned this arrangement in the previous chapter, but it is one of my favorites for getting a good measure of furnished look for very little money. Of course the way you arrange your room depends a great deal on its architectural features. If it is well proportioned, with a good long wall unbroken by odd doors, with windows well spaced, there is no reason you can't place the sofa against the wall and flank it with chairs or a bench on either side. This is a classic arrangement, but it demands side tables of some sort to hold lamps, or else good-looking standing lamps. Also, that grouping must face *something* on the opposite wall—not a fireplace (you are too far from the cheeriness of the fire unless the room is unusually narrow), and not a dining area (you have no feeling of "separation," which is essential for dining in the living room). There are two inexpensive answers to the problem. The first is a wide window or a group of windows that look out on a pretty view; this is an ideal spot (because of the light) for a collection of plants or even a tree if the budget will allow it. I find it makes more financial sense to invest in one really good-looking tall tree for such a window area and fill in as you can with ferns that are not too expensive. You'll get more out of your plant allotment by placing them on a low, benchlike table. These should be simple Parsons-like benches, oil-stained to prevent moisture rings from forming. Lacking the handy touch to make this myself, I once worked out a very good-looking plant bench by staining a fourteen-inch-wide plank cut the length of the group of windows and laying it on a double stack of four used bricks for legs. The combination of brick, simple wood and greenery was sensational.

The second focal point ideally faced by a sofa is a mirrored wall. Mirroring is neither expensive to buy nor a problem to install. Buy the mirrored squares that are self-adhesive. Just peel off the backing and stick them on. It's very easy if you don't get carried away and insist on having wall-to-wall mirroring; then you might require glass cutting, which is not too simple. A small amount of wall space on the sides and bottom is not a tragedy. The mirror does, however, have to start at the ceiling, so start at the top and paste downward. The mirrored squares stick immediately but take a few hours to get really hard; there. efore you can adjust them easily enough should one or two go on unevenly. The thing to do is measure your wall area and consult a salesman at a local mirror or glass shop. He will advise you how many squares you will need. If this mirroring is not available locally, you can order it by mail, along with any number of do-it-yourself decorating items, from Janovic Plaza Paints, 1292 First Avenue, New York, New York 10021. All of the furniture on the opposite wall is reflected in the mirroring and the room consequently looks twice as furnished. In this case I like to center a table, such as the "hall" tables I've mentioned, against the mirrored wall. Hall tables are often found in thrift shops, at first glance hideous, with crackled-varnish finish; but if the lines are fairly simple the table can be antiqued any dark color and will turn out to be elegant.

To double your pleasure from the mirror wall, place a nice big arrangement of dried flowers, wheat or field grass in a basket on your table—the reflection will be an endless pleasure.

If you do decide on the mirrored wall, hang still another mirror over your sofa (unless you are lucky enough to have a lovely painting you would rather use). A good-looking framed mirror can be had for very little money. Begin with an old picture frame. If the gilting is chipped a bit, don't regild it—it's the antique look we are after. Don't let a local mirror dealer talk you into plate glass; tell him what you want is "flashing." This is an extremely cheap mirror that doesn't reflect as accurately as plate glass but has an engagingly wavy appearance that looks exactly like an antique looking glass.

Another happy solution is to face your sofa group with a wall of books, but let me add a word of warning; don't do it unless you are really serious about books and have a sizable collection of them. Nothing is tackier than those modular shelf units that can be arranged any which way with "doodads," sickly potted plants and a pitiful little grouping of books or—especially—exposed hi-fi speakers (a closet fitted with shelves can hold all this electronic paraphernalia and the sound will be just as sweet).

This brings us to television. I know I am a voice crying in the wilderness but I don't think a television set belongs in the living room. Infinitely preferable is a small one in the kitchen for catching the morning news, an even tinier one in the bathroom, or a good-sized one in the bedroom for watching those "don't miss" favorite shows in cozy comfort. If you simply must have one in the living room, I think it is a nice idea to have it at one end of a table desk, which is what I call grouping number three.

Every living room needs some sort of writing table, and here again the thrift shop can come to your rescue. You can usually find a fairly interesting small oblong dining table, which can of course be antiqued any dark color; but an even newer and unusual finish can be achieved by stripping it down to the bare wood, sanding it smooth, and waxing it. This is, admittedly, a bigger job, but there are new super-fast varnish strippers on the market, and if a bit of the dark finish remains in the carving, that's all to the good. Just a few words of caution, though: always work in a well-ventilated area, wear gloves, and cover the floor with several layers of newspapers if you are working indoors.

For desk chairs I like to use rattan when I need a lot of effect for very little cash. They are comfortable if fitted with loose round cushions, and their lightness complements the heaviness of the table. On your table desk avoid any suggestion of a desk "set," those awful penholders, and the like. Paper, pens, paper clips, playing cards (this is a good spot for a game of gin-rummy or backgammon) belong in decorative boxes or in the drawers of the desk. On top you are going to need a good-looking lamp, a generous-sized ashtray, and—if you must—a relatively small television set. I like to place table desks at right angles to the wall. This position is more useful, and it's much pleasanter to face into a room than into a blank wall. Incidentally, this arrangement creates a pleasant spot for two people to have a tray meal; it's also an ideal location for a tray of bar essentials for the next time you have a cocktail party.

If you must find a space for dining in your living room, I suggest a round or square table to break up the rectangular lines of the other furniture. Where to place it? Well, let's assume we are using our first plan, with the sofa at a right angle to the wall flanked by two chairs or a chair and a bench. The area behind the sofa can be attractive for dining if it has easy access to the kitchen. The worst thing you can do is have to traipse through the living room carrying the dirty dishes. In the arrangement of the sofa against the wall, I like to flank the wall opposite my right-angled desk with the dining table. There is still a third plan that I've often used, but it usually requires a fairly large room with a fireplace: place the sofa directly in front of the fireplace facing the fire and flank it with two or three chairs or benches. In this case the dining area can be against the wall in back of the sofa.

This brings us to Thrift Shop Decorating Rule Number Four: *try for a symmetrical balance of your furniture*. Think of it as balancing a scale, equal weight on each side, keeping the room from being lopsided. Think, too, in terms of comfort: a sofa on one wall and two chairs on the other hardly make for a pleasant conversation area. Coffee tables should relate to the furniture they are supposed to service. Nothing irritates me more than those terribly "chi-chi" rooms where an enormous coffee table is placed in the center of a group of furniture at least two yards from any piece. Every time you want to use an ashtray or put down a drink or a coffee cup, you have to get up and walk over to the table! Try to arrange your furniture in as logical a pattern as possible. If, for example, there are two well-spaced windows on one wall, this presents an ideal space for your table and desk at a right angle to the wall. If there is a long blank wall that is convenient to the kitchen, this becomes a perfect spot for a dining area. Move things around until they suit you. The results should be a harmonious, calm, orderly room that works. Above all, don't be afraid of bare spaces. A room needs space to breathe. Far better too little than too much. You can always add, but having to subtract can be an expensive error. Finally, don't crowd your living room with a lot of heavy upholstered furniture. Never—no never—buy one of those dreadful suites of upholstered horrors in the mistaken impression that they are the most comfortable. People are actually more comfortable in fairly light chairs. After all, a chair is to sit in, not to sleep in.

Don't be taken in by advertisements for that low end of all furniture design, the reclining chair. Those monstrosities belong only in bath-dressing rooms, if anywhere at all.

One final word about your living room. You'll notice I have carefully avoided curtains and rugs. We will take up curtains and rugs later, after dealing specifically with dining rooms and bedrooms.

§§§

CHAPTER FIVE

THE DINING ROOM

§§§

NOTHING is nicer or as conducive to a pleasant way of life than to dine nightly at a fully set table in a room designated solely for dining. A dining room is one of our more civilized pleasures as well as an increasingly rare accommodation. Have breakfast on the fly in the kitchen; if you must, lunch catch-as-catch-can; but dinner should be as relaxed and elegant as possible. (Furthermore, children have an amazing way of responding to dinner served in a pleasant, gracious style. Before you can count to five, hands are washed and hair is combed —and who knows, they may begin to act civilized; it's certainly worth a try.)

However, once finished decorating the living room, who on earth has any money for the dining room? Well, here is where we can use a few of our old tricks to great advantage. Fortunately, dining rooms do not require, nor should they have, a great deal of furniture, and there are conventional pieces you don't need at all: a chandelier, for example. The overhead light makes everyone look ghastly, so is best removed at once. Sell it, if it's yours, or pack it away, if it's the landlord's. Another item you don't need in the dining room is a rug. Not only can you get wonderful effects from painting or staining the floors (dark colors only), but you'll save endless hours of cleaning up food from the rugs or carpeting.

What you do need is color and design that will make the most of the sparse furnishing, pretty much limited to a dining-room table and chairs. Here again is the place to "fool the eyes" with

Oak round-top table with pedestal base.

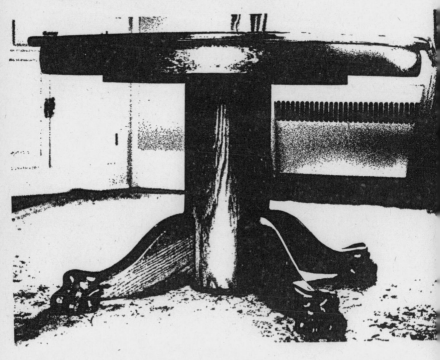

dark colored walls—olive green, warm brown, deep plum, or even a real crimson red—as dining rooms are not often lived in for hours at a stretch. If your dining room opens directly off your living room, the color scheme should have some relation to that of the other room. For example, if you have olive-green living room walls, dark brown would be very good, or if you have a pale-blue living room wall, then plum or crimson red would be attractive. Obviously, you don't want colors that "fight." If the living room is pale yellow, forgo the red or plum in favor of olive or brown.

Again, the focal point, the dining table, is going to look more significant if it is a light color. Thrift Shop Decorating Rule Number Five: *Never buy a dining-room "set."* They are inevitably overpriced and ugly; and the so-called extra pieces —buffet, credenza, side tables, china cabinet—are excessive and unattractive. Even if you find what seems to be a super bargain, forget it; nobody uses sideboards or china cabinets anymore. Look for a good, simple table; and since the room is going to be sparsely furnished, at least at the beginning, a round table will usually give a softer, pleasanter effect. My favorite type is the sturdy, turn-of-the-century golden oak table with a round top and pedestal base. Being "in" again, they are somewhat expensive nowadays, but with a little digging one can be found at a not-too-high price.

Don't worry about the finish; you can paint it or antique it depending on how much time or energy you have. Painting creates the best effect, but a successfully painted table requires that every inch be sanded bone smooth, then a primer coat brushed on and allowed to dry until absolutely slick to the touch. Now a final coat of enamel, and there you are. For dining tables the shiny, crisp look of enamel is my favorite. The antiquing process is easier—sanding is eliminated—you need only the base coat, applied and allowed to dry, then the antiquing stain is wiped on. Here, however, I will make an exception to the rule about antiquing in dark colors. Light blue, light green, or even white, is a better choice than dark for a dining room. As for the chairs, they don't necessarily have to match the table; and, as I have mentioned, dining chairs are the easiest things in the world to find in a thrift shop. Let's assume you are going for broke and painting the walls crimson-red with a white-enameled dining table: try antiquing your chairs in dark red or olive green. Cover the chair seats in a big, splashy print (here's where we add pattern, maybe a floral of red, green, and a touch of yellow). Choose a print you really love because you are going to want to use it for curtains. (More on this later.) If you decide to have curtains, get enough to make a matching round to-the-floor cloth. This is especially effective for parties.

The next illusion you can create for less money than you'd expect is to make a folding screen and cover it with your printed chair fabric. This is easy and cheap. Ask your local lumber dealer to cut three plywood panels for you, each fourteen to sixteen inches wide and at least six feet high. Have him mount them on piano hinges. These swing in two directions. Next cover the screen with flannel, using a staple gun to fasten it, and finally cover with your print—again using a staple gun around the edges of the panels. To make sure the fabric is smooth and taut, start stapling at the top; next, up-end the screen and, allowing a bit of the fabric to hang over to the other side, pull it tight and staple it to the edges, and trim away the excess fabric, making sure you leave enough fabric on top and sides to cover the raw edges of the plywood. The fabric is then trimmed neatly to the edge and the stapled finish is covered by a simple decorative braid held on by plain brass upholstery tacks.

Your screen not only adds a great deal of color and pattern, but it can hide the entrance to the kitchen or break up a long wall by standing in the corner. You can have an elegant dining room with simply your color, table and chairs, and screen. If the budget permits I recommend adding a small chest, but a handsome and durable chest of drawers is frequently expensive. It is therefore wise to wait until you can afford to pick up an interesting antique piece, perhaps at an auction. You will, however, need something to hold a lamp (if you have followed my suggestion and removed the chandelier) and, once again, the faithful Parsons table (unfinished) comes to mind. Finish it to match the dining chairs—after all we can't have too many colors in one room. Later, when you have more cash to spend on an antique chest, the Parsons table can always be repainted to go in the hall or bedroom.

So far I have talked only about using a round table. If you don't find a round one that appeals to you, then look for a square one with rounded corners or an oval. None of these available at your price? Then fall back on a skirted, plywood table top (forty-eight-inch diameter) mounted on a sturdy base (as described earlier in Chapter Three, page 43). If this is your choice, make the skirt of some sort of heavy material like sailcloth or duck, not in white, however, or your room will wind up looking like a restaurant. Pick a paler version of your wall color. To give a few examples, with red walls, a pale pink (or even a very light blue) would be good; with olive green, light blue or yellow; with brown, try light blue, yellow or beige; plum walls are flattered by pale lilac or light blue. You can very easily make squares out of your print fabric for over-cloths; these should be sixty inches square and need only a simple hem—using bias tape for a finishing touch. I recommend making up matching napkins at the same time, but there is no reason not to make a couple of solid-color cloths to go over the heavier undercloth. Try a solid red to go with pink. If you have a bit of red in your print, you can use the red napkins with the print cloth too.

For lighting your dining room, I've already mentioned the single lamp on a side table or chest. Beyond the solitary lamp, I'd use only candles for after-daylight dining. Yes, candle holders can be expensive, even reproduction brass ones, but you can buy attractive glass ones at variety stores for approximately two dollars a pair. Look for utterly plain ones—nothing fancy. New York's Pottery Barn (227 East 60th Street, New York, New York 10022) often has good-looking candlesticks at low and "sale" prices. Another resource is the Fostoria Glass Works (17 East 16th Street, New York, New York 10011). They are happy to get in touch with you about where you can purchase their products. Still a third way to achieve a collection of candle holders is to buy single ones, even in brass and silverplate. They are usually far cheaper than pairs and there is no earthly reason why the candles on your table should match like the animals on Noah's Ark. In fact you can get a far more interesting effect with a variety of heights and shapes. But please stick to relatively simple ones. Those embossed, elaborate ones that some unfortunate Indians or Persians make are death to any room.

Having furnished you with table, tablecloth and candle holders—which can often serve as a centerpiece—we come to china, glassware and serving pieces. I bitterly resent buying things new, with one exception: glasses. For used glasses in thrift shops are usually dreary beyond belief. Personally, I think those wonderful large bubble-shaped wine glasses are great for everything—cocktails, wine, iced tea, milk, you name it. With a little looking you will find them at very low cost. Again, New York's Pottery Barn (see page 68) is an excellent source. For attractive dishes and serving pieces, I suggest two alternatives: one, a basic service of dinner plates, salad plates (that double as dessert plates), and cups and saucers (you don't need bread-and-butter plates or cereal bowls—if your family is addicted to cereal or ice cream, plain glass bowls are cheaper and far more attractive). Thrift Shop Decorating Rule Number Six: *When buying your basic service, be sure to select something utterly simple*. No matter how charming the pattern, you are going to get awfully sick of those roses, poppies and buttercups after you have used them day after day after day. Tiffany (727 Fifth Avenue, New York, N.Y. 10022) has a pattern called "Drab Ware," which is far from drab. It is, rather, completely simple and is available in charming, usable shapes in the color of warm honey. It somehow goes with literally everything and costs about $25 per setting. Or you can select plain white china from Italy. The allure of the plain basic service is that you can mix and match and add to it with interesting antique and other out-of-the-ordinary pieces. Years ago I began collecting antique Wedgwood leaf plates; they look wonderful on the table with my Drab Ware. There are all sorts of dramatic effects that are possible if you start with something that will blend with everything. The only exception I like to make is a really fine reproduction of a classic design, preferably Chinese in extraction. A respected firm recently introduced a reproduction of the famous "Canton ware" from the 18th century. Like all

classics, it goes happily into almost any décor. Write to Mottahedeh and Company, 225 Fifth Avenue, New York, New York
10010, for where to buy it.

As for serving pieces, if your grandmother didn't give you
her sterling silver covered dishes, then white French porcelain
cooking dishes can double for serving dishes. There are all sorts
of shallow oval baking dishes, deep round casseroles, soufflé
dishes, etc., which serve from stove to table handsomely.
Bazaar de la Cuisine, 160 East 59th Street, New York, New
York 10022, carries a fine selection. So do some of the better
thrift shops.

One thing to avoid is the type of porcelain serving dishes that
have so-called "dainty" designs on them. They are distracting
and in dubious taste. Besides, food well prepared and served
creates its own designs.

Finally, what about spoons, forks and knives? I hope some
rich relative left you a handsome sterling silver service; but in
case she or he did not, there are several acceptable substitutes.
If you are determined to have sterling—I don't really blame
you—try to buy it secondhand or at an auction. It's really a
waste to pay retail prices—in my opinion. I've found a good
simple pattern in a quality silverplate acceptable. James Rob-
inson (12 East 57th Street, New York, New York 10019), for
example, makes an utterly simple Old English design with
three-tine forks and pistol-handled knives in plate that I have
been using with pleasure for fifteen years with no sign of wear.
It is a bit more expensive than ordinary plate but nothing like
the cost of sterling.

If you want to spend the least amount of money possible then
by all means get stainless steel. It is wonderfully easy to care
for, and it *is* inexpensive. The one pitfall with stainless steel is

choosing brand and pattern that tries to simulate sterling. It's then robbed of its own virtues. Select a simple modern style, or an Early American classic like the Rat Tail design, or an elegant bamboo effect. Whatever you do, avoid the embossed, so-called "rich" look that advertisers make such a frantic attempt to sell. There is another good-looking choice: plastic-handled stainless steel. I once found a wonderful service with simulated bamboo handles that was immensely good-looking—and dirt cheap. But don't ever put this pattern in the dishwasher —the handles disintegrate.

Well, there you have it—the way to pleasant dining. If you plan well and go about the job of decorating your dining room with a sense of joy and expectation, you'll spend many a contented hour there entertaining your friends and family in an atmosphere that is truly conducive to a happier life.

§§

CHAPTER SIX

THE BEDROOM

§§

SURPRISINGLY enough, the bedroom is probably the easiest room in the house in which to get the most effect for the least money. There is one item on which you simply cannot economize: your bedspring and mattress. You can, however, forgo a headboard. Settle for the best box spring and mattress you can afford and then have them mounted on legs for very little extra cost. Most stores that sell beds will do this for you. One other point on the bedding question: look for sales at bedding stores. Most stores of this type have so-called "Super Clearance" sales every few weeks. Look for a good name brand and get it at the best possible price.

How do you go about decorating a bedroom? That depends on what kind of bedroom and who's going to occupy it. Let's take the worst type first—the little cubbyhole that is quaintly described by real estate brokers as a "sleeping alcove." The first thing is to try to screen off this corner from the living quarters. I once knew a famous decorator who had the courage to place a full-size bed right in the living room. It must have cost a fortune as it was quilted all over, headboard, legs and all, with what was obviously a very expensive print. I regret to say I still didn't like it. So, unless you are a very brave soul indeed, I think you will be more comfortable if you conceal your sleeping area. The easiest and cheapest way to do this is to buy three or four louvered panels at least fourteen inches wide at the local lumber yard and have them mounted on the same piano hinges I mentioned in Chapter Five, or find a set of louvers at the local junkyard or thrift shop. These can then be either stained or spray-painted. If you decide on the latter, it is a good idea to paint it the color of the walls. In cramped quarters too many colors are just too "much," period. They make the room look jumbled and messy. The same goes for the walls of your alcove—never paint them a different color from the rest of your room. If you do, the alcove literally leaps out and calls attention to its smallness.

Obviously, in such a cubbyhole you are not going to have much room for furniture. If you can be comfortable on a thirty-three-inch bed, it's going to look a lot better than the usual thirty-nine-inch width. As for covering, it should in the alcove situation be designed to promote quick and easy bed-making, especially if you have little time to spend "neating up" your apartment before leaving for work. One method is to have a very simple, tailored "dust ruffle," (no pleats or ruffles, however, just a simple kick pleat in each corner) made of a fairly sturdy material—sailcloth (there I go again), velveteen or duck—in a shade that is as close to the wall color as possible. Here we reverse our principle of using light-colored covers for a more furnished look. Since the area is small, we want the furniture to blend into the space and not contrast with it. Now, after you have your dust ruffle base, add a simple matching hemmed spread that will cover the mattress to the top of the dust ruffle; that is, usually about ten inches over the side of the bed. In other words, measure the top of the bed, plus the drop on the sides to just beyond the top of the box spring. Then add a matching pillow sham and a comfortable blanket or quilt. Your "sleeping" pillow, in pillow case, can be stowed away in a closet. Plan on using a fitted bottom sheet on the bed. At night all you have to do is fold up the top coverlet, add a top sheet and your regular "sleeping" pillow, and pull up the comforter or blanket—and you're off to pleasant dreams. In the morning it takes only seconds to fold up the top sheet and stash it away in a closet, along with your service pillow. On goes the matching coverlet, the decorative pillow and the neatly folded blanket or comforter, and your room is in order.

This may sound a little stark if what you are longing for is a cozy, luxurious bedroom, but the tiny sleeping alcove just can't take too much going on. You can, however, add a lot of "look" for very little money by hanging a large mirror (see living room chapter for suggestions on how to have a great mirror for a tiny price) to the wall facing the living room, and—if you're lucky enough to have a window—a good-looking plant, say a small palm tree, adds greatly to the warmth of the room without taking up too much space. One of my favorite tricks for alcove bedrooms is to have a big basket filled with favorite magazines. You are also going to need a small table for a lamp and perhaps a clock, a book, or a favorite photograph or two. Small tables, fortunately, are not hard to find at thrift shop prices. I have often found in such emporia a piano bench, in a good, extra-simple shape, enameled it shiny black or dark blue, and used it with great success as a bedside table. A piano bench is just about the right height, and in cramped quarters the space (under the seat) that once was for sheet music can hold all sorts of papers or writing materials. One word of caution, however: if the finish has "cracked" and is not smooth, it must be sanded before enameling. Antiquing, the alternative that I have mentioned so often before, doesn't look right for piano benches. Don't ask me why—it just doesn't.

One last word of advice about alcove bedrooms: try for a comforter or blanket as luxurious as possible—it takes away the "poor" look at once. One of the most successful comforters I ever made was simplicity itself; for one side I used a single bed sheet in a tiny floral pattern that I particularly liked, then for the reverse side, velveteen in its exact size. My color combination was olive green velveteen and a print of greens, lilac and pinks. Since the length of velveteen was not as wide as the sheet, I used one full width for the center and split another length for the sides. The velveteen was then stitched together on the reverse side. The sheet and velveteen were sewn together on one side and at the top (on the reverse side, of course). The resulting "bag" effect was turned inside out and stuffed evenly with polyester fill. Leaving one side and one end open makes this an easier job. I then turned in the raw edges of the remaining sides and blind-stitched them by hand. To keep the "fill" from "shifting," I tacked it down at six-inch intervals with small grosgrain bows of the same olive green. The result was luxury itself, and I've since made literally hundreds in all sorts of patterns. I've done some for male clients with solid velveteen combined with gingham check or plaid, with small buttons substituted for the bows.

The alcove to the regular bedroom is a step up in convenience right from the start. Let's begin with the usual not-too-distinguished bedroom found in most apartments and new houses. It is, naturally, a great deal easier if your bedroom has an eighteen-foot ceiling, a fireplace, and French doors that open onto a balcony, but most of us are not that lucky. So the first thing is to try to get some interest into the room itself. Since a bed or beds are a necessity, we'll start with the sleeping surface. Personally, I hate king-size beds; they seem so out of proportion. Queen-size, if you like, but not king-size, unless your room is absolutely huge.

You can give your bedroom a great deal of interest by the way the beds are treated. Personally, I think dust ruffles are an absolute necessity. As I have already mentioned box springs and mattresses on legs are the least expensive way of providing the necessary sleeping arrangement, but the legs should be covered, and a dust ruffle is the simplest way to do the job. Fortunately, this device is easy to make and inexpensive to have made. You simply measure the length and width of your box spring and the length from the top of the box spring to the floor. Now, allowing two inches extra up-and-down for hemming, cut a length of fabric exactly double the measurement of box-spring length plus width. The fabric is then gathered to the measurements you have obtained and stitched to a plain muslin base or to an old sheet. Almost any fabric can be used, from inexpensive white muslin to gingham to your favorite print. Now you can either match or contrast a blanket cover finished with a plain or ruffled edge; if plain, it's a nice idea to bind the edge with bias tape for a professional look. Add pillow shams, ruffled or with a two-inch flange finish and you are on your way to a very custom effect.

No headboard? Nothing to worry about. One of the most

effective bedrooms I ever designed had a one-inch strip of plywood nailed directly over the back of the bed at ceiling height. The blanket-cover fabric was then gathered to double fullness, long enough to reach from ceiling to floor, and stapled to the plywood strip. This edge was then finished with a simple braid trim, again stapled in place. This of course is only one way to get some visual interest into your sleeping arrangements.

Very often thrift shops and auctions have unusual headboards at not too high a price. These are what I call "Elsie De Wolfe" painted bedroom pieces. They are admittedly hard to find, so grab anything you can get. The prices are still low and they are going to become tomorrow's collectors' items. Usually painted in delicate colors, often in creamy white, these bedroom pieces are decorated with fragile sprays of flowers, ribbons and such. The headboards are frankly for a woman's room, but the occasional chests often look fine in less feminine quarters. If you are interested in this type of furniture, you might want to check your local library for any books by Elsie De Wolfe; the few that she wrote are lavish with photographs.

Still another choice for headboards that are even less expensive are old-fashioned iron beds. With brass bed prices out of sight, I've found iron beds a happy substitute. I like to paint them a glossy black or white, though once I changed one to a deep scarlet for a man's room, and did the blanket cover and dust ruffle in a wool tattersall check of black, gray and red. It depends on the room and who will sleep in it.

Bedrooms should be comfortable, and the easiest way I know to is to add a few upholstered pieces. For some reason loveseats seem to be cheaper than sofas or chairs in thrift and upholstery shops. Maybe it's because they are not as desirable for living rooms. They are perfect for bedrooms. Add a loveseat covered in a good color, plus one or two cushions in a compatible print, and right away you give your bedroom a really finished look. If you can, place your bed or beds on your longest wall and the loveseat on the opposite wall. I like to add a coffee table, if nothing more than a luggage stand topped by a simple tray. This makes a lovely place to have that first cup of coffee, or even a nightcap.

Another trick for giving a bedroom a luxurious look is to use a pair of covered tables by the bed or beds. As previously mentioned, these are usually round tops of plywood, thirty-six-inch round, mounted on any sturdy base about twenty-eight or twenty-nine inches high. On occasion I've used nail kegs. Such tables are then covered with to-the-floor cloths in any fairly substantial fabric, and then, to be really practical, topped with a square (or round) of matching or contrasting fabric that can be removed for easy laundering. You can top your table with glass; but plate glass is a bit expensive and the non-plate glass breaks too easily.

To measure your table for cloths, simply add double the height to the diameter of the table top. In other words, a thirty-six-inch table twenty-nine inches high would require two lengths of forty-five to fifty-inch-wide material ninety-four inches long, or approximately six yards. The diameter of the table is obtained by measuring across at the widest point. A center strip is cut to the measurements required, in this case ninety-four inches, then two half-moons of the remaining yardage are cut to form the sides of the cloth. If you are not an experienced home sewer, Simplicity Patterns has wonderfully easy-to-follow tablecloth patterns. For the top cloth, you will need a forty-five-inch square (or circle) of cloth, plus one inch for hemming. I like to finish the edges in bias tape in a matching or contrasting color.

So far we have not touched on bedroom color schemes. Again, as mentioned earlier, you have first to decide on the type of person you are and what colors appeal to you most. Generally speaking I prefer calm color schemes for bedrooms. After all a bedroom is a retreat from the outside world, not a display area. I once did a bedroom for a young dress designer who lived a hectic, high-paced life; what he wanted in his sleeping quarters was peace and quiet. We settled on a color scheme of beige and white. Sounds dull? Well, it was one of the loveliest rooms you can imagine—and we created it at thrift-shop prices. Since the floor was in rather bad condition, we covered the entire surface in rush matting. The walls were painted the color of bamboo, and the curtains, blanket cover, and dust ruffle were of white muslin, at a dollar and five cents a yard. The bedstead itself was an old iron one we found for sixteen dollars and painted a warm beige. The curtains were lined with tiny print in brown, beige and white, picked up at a mill-end store for seventy cents a yard. But our real find was two tea chests, the original shipping crates used for wholesale shipments of tea from the Orient. They actually cost only two dollars each, and their wonderful square shapes bound in strips of tin were perfect bedside tables. The Japanese lettering on them was a nice decorative effect. Now I don't claim that tea boxes can be found on any corner, but if you are interested in the idea, I suggest you look up some Oriental food importers; visit or write to them and ask if they have any shipping crates or baskets that they would sell. I've bought some wonderful baskets this way for prices that are so low it's almost embarrassing.

But back to our dress designer's room. We added a small sofa slipcovered in beige duck and a pair of those folding captain's chairs in natural wood and white canvas. An up-ended rattan stool served as a coffee table, and for that bit of snap that every room needs, a pair of Chinese ginger jar lamps in shiny black. The final accent was a group of huge ferns, arranged on a pebble-filled tin baker's tray (bought at a restaurant supply store), which we enameled in glistening black.

Sky blue is another almost neutral color that makes an effective background for any other color, as well as having a calming, restful effect itself. I'm especially addicted to blue walls, particularly in combination with a floral print for curtains. Bedrooms, along with dining rooms, can use the splash of color of a good print. Also, a floral print produces the kind of casual, garden effect that so many people like in personal living quarters.

Here are some of the color schemes I've found pleasant for bedrooms; again, it's your personal choice, but these combinations seem to work well.

The beige, white and bamboo scheme described in this chapter.

Sky-blue walls with bed covers of deep forest green, curtains and accent cushions in a mixed floral of blue, green, purple and pink.

Pale lilac walls, bed covers in a tiny sprig print of blue, yellow, green and pink. Upholstered pieces in deep aubergine. Curtains of the same print as the bedcovers.

White walls, red-lacquered iron bed, curtains and bed covers of tattersall check in black, gray and red. Natural straw rug, upholstered pieces in same clear red as the bed.

Clear yellow walls, curtains and bed covers in a splashy print of yellows, pinks, greens and blues. Upholstered pieces in deep green.

Dark olive green walls, bed covers and upholstered pieces in plain white, floor stained very dark and then highly polished.

Dark brown walls, bed covers and curtains in white or clear lemon yellow.

Do you have a guest bedroom? You do? I hope it's not like too many guest rooms, a collection area for all the junk in the house. I hope it is, instead, like the one in the house of a friend

Padded coat hanger with pomander ball.

of mine who has little money but great taste—and a feeling for good living. I love being a guest in her house. The guest room walls are sky blue, the blanket covers, dust ruffle and curtains are made from white sheeting edged in Irish lace. The furniture is nondescript but it has been enameled in bright, shiny white. There is a lovely, cozy old afghan in pinks and purples at the foot of an inviting chaise longue. A good selection of books and magazines is stacked on a generous-sized bedside table, along with a workable lamp. The closets are blessedly empty, except for a group of nice padded hangers and a fragrant pomander ball. On a side table there is an ice bucket (always filled), a bowl of fruit, and a thermos of orange juice, plus a clock that works. In a drawer of the bedside table are the little necessities it's so easy to forget: aspirin, safety pins, cotton pads, a bottle of skin freshener. Because this is not a lavish house, one must share the single bathroom, but it is always neat and inviting. In the bath there is a "guest" terry robe and a pair of straw slippers, just in case you forgot yours. In essence, provisions for guests show that the hostess really cares, and that, my friends, is what decorating is all about.

A few final thoughts on bedrooms. Here is a place for your memorabilia, favorite pictures, family photographs, etc. But do keep them organized. "Organized clutter" is the term a friend of mine coined. No matter what the color scheme, or the fabric, or the furniture—if the room is disorganized with a lopsided arrangement of ornaments, pictures, odd pillows and so on, it will look dreadful. Keep working with what one great decorator called your "tablescapes," until you have the look you want.

Lastly, bedroom closets are part of your room. I like to paint their walls and shelves the same colors as the bedroom walls. If you can't afford any of those padded hangers, you can spray-paint wooden hangers in one of the colors of the room. No wire hangers, please, and remember, everybody, keep your closet neat—it's part of the look.

§§§

CHAPTER SEVEN

THE KITCHEN

§§§

THE big problem with decorating a kitchen is that you have to cook in it; and—let's face it—even the most dedicated gourmet will have to admit that cooking is a messy procedure. The *duck à l'orange* or the *steak au poivre* has to be flamed with brandy, and *voilà!* The drama and the taste are great, but the wallpaper is ruined. Even everyday, meat-and-potatoes, bacon-and-eggs cooking gives off smoke and fumes, and the even row of charming copper-bottomed pots that look so enchanting when shown in magazines lose their charm if they are tarnished in less than a week (and they will be). Unless you are really crazy about polishing copper, it's best to forget how great they would look hanging over your stove top.

Another thing that never fails to irritate me is the illustration of the sunny windowsill filled with growing herbs, the whole thing framed with charming ruffled curtains. The chance of plants thriving in kitchen fumes and curtains staying fresh for more than a week is about nil.

Now that I have sourly said what you can't do, let's take a more positive approach and see what *can* be done to make your kitchen as attractive as any room in the house, for the least possible cash. The very first thing to consider is ventilation. The nicest colors and fabrics are a waste if the kitchen isn't ventilated. So, before you spend a cent on décor, install the best ventilating system you can afford. The cheapest (and, to my mind, quite satisfactory) way to get things moving is to install an inexpensive ventilating fan in the kitchen window. The most luxurious way is to install over the stove a ventilating hood that exhausts to the outside. In between, the only thing to do (especially if you don't have a window) is to have a hood over the stove that catches the dirt and grease in a removable filter. All three methods work; and what's more, both ventilating fans and filter hoods are often available secondhand. Once again (as with buying a sofa) try the repair shops (electrical this time, of course, not upholstery). The ventilating fans are easier to find, and if you do have a window, this is the cheapest and easiest way to solve the problem. One practical note about any ventilating system is that it must be kept clean. Fan blades should be wiped off with ammonia water, and filters must be washed frequently. Otherwise the whole point is lost.

Now let's get on with what you can do to make the kitchen look great. Your best buy is paint, washable paint in a non-kitchen color. Most people think only in terms of white and yellow, or possibly blue, for kitchen walls. The result is so pallid that the poor kitchen needs copper pots, plants and all kinds of doodads to keep it from looking like a dentist's office. Think for a minute about *color* for kitchens. I once painted a small apartment kitchen a deep, shiny brown; the appliances were the usual apartment-house white, and the cabinets were standard white metal. Suddenly they lost their ordinary look completely. The crisp brown and white was a smash. I covered the ordinary ceiling fixture with a Japanese lantern in natural rice paper with black trim. It cost three dollars at Azuma, a Japanese gift shop, at 790 Lexington Avenue, New York, New York 10022. White linen towels stitched in brown that I made myself, a white vinyl floor (you can use those self-sticking vinyl tiles—it's amazingly easy), a natural bamboo blind at the window, and a basket on the counter for onions and potatoes added the final touches to that little kitchen. No gimmicks, no expensive curtains, no tricks—just color and common sense.

Or how about dark navy blue walls? You can get the same effect: just substitute a white-painted bamboo blind and maybe a white ironstone bowl for the potatoes and onions. Incidentally, though ironstone prices have gone up lately, it's still possible to get some good buys, and they always make for good decoration. (In case you are not familiar with ironstone, it is the heavy, white stoneware made in the latter half of the nineteenth century.) Plain and completely free of the curse of "decoration," the pitchers and bowls are great for flowers; and I love the look of the plates for everyday table settings.

Dark walls simply don't appeal to you? Well, that doesn't mean you can't make a strong statement with color in your kitchen. If you really want a yellow kitchen, fine, but make it a good, sharp lemon-peel yellow. You'll have to fight for it: most paint stores will insist that their anemic, so-called "sunshine yellow" will look darker when on the wall—it won't. It will only look washed out. If you can't get your local paint store to cooperate, write Janovic Plaza Paints (see page 55), who will ship any color you want (*without* an argument).

Still another color that's wonderful in a kitchen is a true sky blue—not that hideous grayed blue that paint stores call "French blue." French? The French would sue them! What you want is the clear, bright blue of a summer sky; it's a splendid kitchen color.

I like to use one strong color, then lots of white in a kitchen; and since I strongly believe that anyone on a limited budget is out of his mind to buy elaborate appliances, the appliances usually provide this plain white. Even given an unlimited budget, I would shy away from avocado-green refrigerators and decorator-style stoves. I have spent a lot of time as the poorhouse guest of some very rich people, and I have yet to see a colored refrigerator or a fancied-up stove in one of their kitchens. In fact, if you are a true thrift-shop hound, as I am, you wouldn't dream of buying refrigerators, stoves or washing machines brand new. Good refurbished ones are usually available, too, at appliance stores or through the "Household Goods For Sale" column in your local newspaper.

This leads me to kitchen cabinets. Americans are cabinet-happy—they have been sold on the idea that every available inch of kitchen wall space must be covered by a cabinet. No matter if the one over the refrigerator makes it impossible to clean the refrigerator top and anything stored in it unobtainable except by ladder. Or that the cabinets are built so close to the stove that it is impossible to clean the remaining quarter-inch of space between; meanwhile, food spills accumulate—if you think they don't, have an appliance man pull out the stove. I guarantee it will make you sick. Another pet peeve of mine is the cabinet built just far enough from the ceiling to accumulate grease and dirt, but too close to get a cleaning rag between cabinet and ceiling. Why, oh why, do they do it? If you own your own house, consider how many cabinets you really need and ponder the cleaning problem at the same time. All those cabinets have to be washed out from time to time, or you will certainly be rewarded by a host of small, many-footed visitors.

If you live in an apartment where the cabinets are of the metal variety, examine them carefully. They are usually screwed to the wall and can be easily removed; take out the cabinets you don't need and store them in the basement. You'll be amazed how spacious the kitchen will look. I once removed all of the cabinets in my own tiny apartment kitchen and it seemed to double in size. What did I do for storage? I didn't—I simply hung all the pots and pans on the wall, with the exception of my big French stew pot, which sat decoratively on the stove. All food was stored in the refrigerator—which fortunately was of ample size—or in air-tight containers that sat on a handy small table. I really enjoyed that kitchen; it was a breeze to keep clean, and it really worked. You might consider the idea. After all, the best cooks in the world—the French—do not have any cabinets at all in their traditional kitchens. Believing that pots and pans sour if closed up in cabinets, they hang cooking utensils on racks where they can "air out" from one cooking to the next. It's not a bad idea.

As a matter of record (while I'm still on the subject of cabinets), one of the best-looking kitchens I ever designed had only a bare minimum of cabinets; all the cooking equipment either was hung on the wall or sat on the open shelves of a wonderful old armoire which we had picked up for $45, a bargain because it had no doors. Antiqued dark blue and placed against a sky blue wall, it was the focal point of the room.

As for other kitchen furniture, I think a table and chairs for an early morning cup of coffee, or for breakfast, for that matter, are a must if you have any space at all. Since most of the so-called kitchen sets are hideous beyond belief, it pays to use a little thrift shop ingenuity. Wrought-iron garden tables and chairs are sometimes a good buy, especially if they are in need of a paint job, an easy matter to solve with the new spray enamels. Old-fashioned square or oblong wooden tables can be unearthed with a little luck—try country auctions if you have a chance. Scrubbed down and left to their own weathered good looks, these are great kitchen tables. Chairs are less of a problem—almost any clean-lined straight chairs can be spray painted in a good enamel finish, and it doesn't matter a bit if they don't match the table. I've used old, natural-finish wooden tables with white enameled chairs for a great effect. Put that big ironstone bowl I was talking about in the center of the table.

One of the most important decisions to make concerning your kitchen is what should be on the floor. Whoever dreamed up the idea of kitchen carpeting should be made to clean it up every day for a year. Maybe that would reinforce the idea that it is ugly, impossible to clean, and a general nuisance. Fortunately, kitchen carpeting seems to be a diminishing trend, for which we can all be thankful.

What you put on your floor depends on what's already on it. I know Americans are absolutely sold on the idea of covering the floor with something, but for generations we existed with plain, uncovered wooden floors in the kitchen. If you have an old house where the existing floor covering is badly worn, you might consider ripping it up and sanding the floor down to the bare wood. Apply a coat of clear finish (the new ones are tough, long-lasting, and washable), and there you are: a good-looking floor for a lot less money than you thought.

Personally, I love the look of wooden floors in a kitchen and consider them an asset, not a drawback. But what if the floor under the existing one is concrete? Paint will hold up very well. This type of paint admittedly does not come in the world's most exciting colors, but a shiny black or dark red floor (and it *does* come in these colors) can fit into most kitchen color schemes.

If you simply can't do anything but cover your floor, then I suggest that asphalt tile in a random brick pattern is very effective. It is much cheaper than vinyl, and to my mind very attractive. It comes in squares of four "bricks" and can easily be laid by the amateur craftsman. I use it repeatedly in both the white-washed and natural red finish, and have found it both decorative and practical.

Next up the economic scale is vinyl, and of course it is practical. But please keep it plain—fancied up and made to look like mosaic or inlaid with gold, it is just awful. Plain white (my favorite), dark blue, black, dark red are all good; but those garish "decorator-style" (there's that curse again) patterns that are often glowingly described as "a new dimension in luxury" are only a new dimension in bad taste.

Now that the floor question is settled, let's look up to the ceiling. Up there is usually a very ugly white, bowl-shaped light fixture that sheds a harsh light over everything, making anyone so unfortunate as to be in the kitchen look like Whistler's mother or father. Unless you really want to look twenty years older, get rid of the ceiling fixture. There are three places where you need good light in the kitchen: over the stove, over the sink, and over your work counter. If you have a hood over your stove, it probably has a light in it; if so, all to the good. For the remaining areas (and over the stove if it's hood-less), install spotlights that pinpoint the light right where you need it most. Once again, I always buy these second hand at an electrical repair shop. If you run into difficulty locating them, I'll let you in on the key secret in thrift shop decorating: Try to win over the various tradespeople you need to help you. Make friends, take time to visit for a few minutes, take an interest in the business. I confess I've even brought homemade cookies to my favorite upholsterer. Don't laugh, it works—he will call you whenever he finds what you want. And, quite honestly, you'll get a better price. I know, it's worked for me for years.

Once you have settled your practical work light, consider a simple but good-looking lamp for your kitchen table; its soft glow is a lot more attractive for kitchen suppers than overhead lighting. Kitchen lamps should not look like living-room lamps; try a candlestick base of brass or pewter with a linen or gingham shade, or a glass reproduction of an oil lamp. (Speaking of candle holders, unelectrified, they make effective kitchen decorations, and are very handy for those moments when the lights blow out, which seems to happen at least once a month during hot weather thunderstorms, to say nothing of creating a great effect when you want to give a kitchen candlelight supper.)

Your choice of cooking utensils can be of great decorative value to your kitchen. No, it doesn't have to be copper. The French enameled ironware comes in marvelous kitchen colors: clear blue, burnished red, strong yellow. The initial cost is not cheap but the cost of sleazy cookware added to the price of so-called kitchen "decorations" will equal the price of some decent pots and pans. A plain white crock of wooden spoons and French wire whisks looks fine on a kitchen counter, where they are best left to "air out," not stashed away in a dark drawer. Buy yourself one of those wonderful glass Chemex coffee pots and leave it out to air after each using. The simple

A crock for holding cooking utensils.

glass beaker shape is good design, and it makes great coffee too. Keep your wooden chopping block out on the counter where it is used, and your rolling pin, too, perhaps in a big mixing bowl.

I happen to love plain white linen dish towels, maybe stitched in red, brown or dark blue; they are inexpensive if you make your own, and certainly they are simplicity itself to make. You don't even have to own a sewing machine. Above all, when you are adding the finishing touches to your kitchen, remember that the familiar kitchen clutter is death to good looks. Get rid of gadgets that hang on the wall and do nothing but distract the eye and collect dirt. Have you ever looked at the blade of that electric can opener? Filthy is the only word. Also to be thrown out are all those messy pot scrubbers, cleaning pads and sponges. Paper towels or a good sturdy dish cloth kept well rinsed with lots of hot water are greatly to be preferred.

In essence, let honesty be your policy. If you really like to cook with herbs, then you know it's dishonest to store them over the stove where they rapidly lose their flavor. They don't look "cute," they just look foolish. Put the herbs in the refrigerator and leave the wall over the stove mercifully free of "darling" little hanging shelves. This is not to say a kitchen has to be utterly stark. If you happen to find a wonderful old wall clock in the thrift shop, hang it in your kitchen. But get it working first—then it means something.

More than anything else, avoid the so-called kitchen accessories beloved by department store gift shops. The decorated canisters, the framed mats, the "kitchen" ashtrays. Substitute simple glass or stoneware crocks with tight-fitting cork tops, or old-fashioned plain "canning" jars with glass lids and snap-on metal bands. Forgo the printed mottos for something that has meaning for you: a favorite poster, framed, or an old grocery ad

(I have one, dated 1931; sirloin is advertised at nineteen cents a pound!). Or perhaps a crayon drawing your child did at school. As for ashtrays, I like big ironstone saucers and plenty of big kitchen matches.

Finally, fill a big pitcher with daisies or zinnias, if it's summer, with dried wheat in winter, and look around you. I guarantee you'll love the results!

§§§

CHAPTER EIGHT

THE BATHROOM

§§§

BATHROOMS present the problem of lack of space more dramatically than any other room in the house. Unless you are either lucky or rich (or both), you are probably contending with a room roughly the size of a shoebox, counting yourself fortunate if you have a window.

There are all sorts of ways of creating the illusion of space, but most are based on reflection. You can mirror a wall with the inexpensive squares mentioned earlier. You can use bright shiny paints (again, reflection). Or you can even wallpaper a bath with aluminum foil; honestly, I've done it, and the effect is terrific. Common kitchen foil is simply glued to the wall in strips.

And now we come to the biggest space maker of all, and it doesn't cost a cent. In a word, neatness. A small bathroom that presents a jumble of varicolored towels, cluttered medicine cabinets, worn bars of soap, and a tub whose edges are filled with bottles and jars is a decorating nightmare. Use one color for all your towels, if you can. I once did a minuscule bathroom for a small apartment. The walls were lacquered shiny white and the towels were quilted white terry cloth bound in green. We added a pot of fern and bars of green soap. Believe me, it looked great.

Now let me tell you about these towels. You make them yourself from a double layer of the regular terry cloth sold in most department and fabric stores. Cut them to the size you want, then quilt the two layers together with a quilting attachment (simply a bar that attaches to your sewing machine). I myself prefer straight quilting to criss-cross; it is also easier to do. Then bind the edges of the towel with bias tape in any color you like. They are the most luxurious towels I've ever seen, and the cost is well below the same quality in commercial towels. Incidentally, it pays to shop around for terry cloth. It is frequently the favorite "special" in mill-end shops.

I don't like bathroom carpeting—it makes the room look even smaller and it is difficult to keep clean. And as for all those plush toilet-seat cover sets that are supposed to dress up your bath, avoid them like the plague. They are ugly to start with and wind up looking frowzy in just a few weeks, besides needing almost constant laundering to keep looking halfway decent. Invest instead in a few unusual accessories, and here's where you can do very well at auctions and antique and junk shops. A tortoiseshell box for hairpins, an old glass for toothbrushes —just one or two such things to add interest. Just make sure they are utilitarian; bathrooms don't need and have no room for useless objects.

If you are lucky enough to have a bathroom window, a couple of plants can add a great deal of decoration for very little money. If there simply is not enough room down below, try a hanging basket. Ferns do especially well in a bathroom—it's the humidity they thrive on.

Shower curtains and window curtains come next in the list of bathroom problems. Once again, if space is the issue, think carefully before buying those matching sets in busy prints or garish colors. You can make your own shower curtains, you know; they couldn't be simpler. The best-looking ones, in my opinion, are simply plain duck in any color, especially white. You simply measure the width of the bath area to be covered and the length from the rod to about five inches below the tub rim. Cut the panels the necessary length plus three inches for hems on all four sides. Stitch the panels together and finish the inside with pinking shears or a flat seam. Hem the curtain with a three-inch hem on all four sides. Now, fasten brass rings to the top of the curtain, using heavy duty thread, and there you are. Just be sure your rings are the right size for your rod—they must be big enough to slide easily. About rods: I like to remove most ordinary shower rods; they are unsightly and cumbersome. Install one of the tension curtain rods in a brass finish, just far enough from the ceiling to allow the rings to slide. The effect is much tidier and smoother-looking than a heavy rod fourteen or sixteen inches from the ceiling. You can do this, however, only if you make your own shower curtains, or your bathroom ceiling is uncommonly low. Store-bought curtains are usually too short.

Now for the window. Bathroom windows should be kept simple. Usually it's best to match window curtains to the shower curtain (that space problem again); but there is an alternative that I like better, in most instances. That is to "curtain" the window with a roll-up bamboo shade. They are available at Oriental import shops, or department and variety stores, and they have the triple advantage of being extremely attractive, inexpensive, and easy to clean. Any variety of rattan, wicker, or bamboo looks right in bathrooms, I've found. Baskets for soap, for towels, even small rattan stools or baskets up-ended and used as tables (if there's room) can be very successful.

Space is not the only factor in decorating bathrooms. There's your personality to consider. If you see your bathroom only as a quickly-escaped-from, functional part of your house, then keep it fresh and simple; on the other hand, if you like to luxuriate in a tub of fragrant hot water, then give yourself something to look at, an antique mirror over the wash basin or a flowered ceiling. In a small bathroom is about the only place where I recommend a patterned wallpaper—in fact, it's the only place I recommend using wallpaper at all. One of the prettiest small bathrooms I've ever seen was incredibly small, but it did have a window. The walls were painted a very pale, shiny pink. The ceiling was papered in a trellis design of pink, green and white, and the towels were white with pink binding. The shower curtain was plain white duck, and a white painted rattan shade served as a window treatment. A pot of pink African violets thrived in the light and high humidity. The owner, a young artist, adored spending a luxurious half hour daily in the tub, tracing the airy trellis pattern with her eyes.

Perhaps, however, you are lucky and have space to burn, in an old house built when people thought in terms of feet, not inches. If so, then you can really create an interesting bath for very little money. In the first place, most large bathrooms have windows and windows mean light; therefore you can go in for more color, pattern and variety. More light means more plants will prosper there, too, and plants are the easiest way to bring glamour into the plainest room.

In a big, old-fashioned bathroom very likely there is a big, old-fashioned tub sitting grandly on its own sturdy feet. Don't be in too much of a rush to replace it—it has great decorative value. Paint the outside instead in a color matching or, preferably, contrasting with, your walls.

What fun in a big bathroom to go all out for a feeling of great luxury with very little cash. David Hicks, the famous English decorator, has given us a whole new concept in bathroom furnishing. He frequently adds a chaise longue or even a sofa to his super-luxurious baths. There's always a rug and a dressing table, flowering plants around, and the effect is marvelous.

I recently redecorated a bath for a young couple who had moved into a big, roomy Victorian house. The bath was charming, with large dormer windows and loads of light. The outside of an old clawfoot tub was painted a dark navy blue in contrast to the light blue walls. A dressing-table area was created by building a plywood frame around the wash basin and the frame covered in dark blue vinyl. A tightly gathered skirt of white muslin was made to hang from the edge of the frame to the floor. The skirt was first gathered on a plain band (three times the width of the area, to assure fullness), then the band was stapled in place to the edge of the frame, and finished off with a decorative braid, again in solid white. Since the room really was big, I added a rug—a real rug, not bathroom carpeting. It was a nice, faded, old Oriental, small but good-looking, in a mélange of colors but mostly deep red, cream and blue. Wicker stools held big white towels edged in deep maroon. A small wicker chair (found for fourteen dollars) was sprayed white to add the finishing touch.

There are many small things for little cost that can add glamour to a bathroom. Soap, for example. Fragrant soaps can add a nice touch of luxury and they really don't cost that much more. Most department stores and specialty shops have their own brand of fragrant soaps on special sale in boxes of six or eight at least twice a year. Bar for bar they cost just pennies more than supermarket soaps. A stack of fresh washcloths near the basin is not only a great convenience, but also adds to the feeling of luxury. And, finally, try to keep one fresh flower in a small vase somewhere in the room. I know a girl who uses an empty perfume bottle for this, and the effect is charming.

As for bathroom color schemes, I believe in keeping them simple. Again, that space problem: it takes a decidedly baronial room to accommodate more than three colors. For very small baths, I like to stick to one color plus white, and in a large bath, two or three colors. Any of the pastel shades—pale pink, pale blue, yellow, and so forth—are pretty with white, but have you considered beige? This is a wonderful background color for almost any room, but I have begun to like it a great deal for baths. It looks marvelous with white towels, green plants, wicker and rattan, all the things I've become addicted to for bathrooms.

And of course you won't want to forget the sandalwood soap.

§§

CHAPTER NINE

PATIOS, PORCHES AND TERRACES

§§§

IF you are lucky enough to have some real outdoor space, then you are very fortunate. You certainly should make the most of it.

Unfortunately those lovely terraces you see photographed in magazines usually cost at least a couple of thousand dollars to accomplish. What to do about it? Well, a little thrift shop ingenuity is in order. Let me describe a few examples that may be of interest and a bit of help.

Problem number one: a charming, small, flagstone terrace under a big oak tree outside a rather formal Georgian house. The interior we had managed to pull together with yards of flowered chintz and lots of painted furniture. When we arrived at the terrace, there was simply no money left, or very little. Certainly not enough to buy even thrift shop furniture. We did have left over some scraps of fabric—a yard of one kind, a few yards of another. We decided to decorate the terrace with pillows. Big, fat foam-rubber cushions twenty inches square were covered with whatever fabric we still had. They were all sturdy cottons, and we simply made plain zippered covers. These we stacked—two here, two there, wherever they looked effective. Naturally, they had to be protected against the elements; we solved that problem by keeping three large plastic garbage bags handy in a kitchen drawer. A threatening sky and the pillows are stashed away in a hall closet until the storm in over. And why not? Who is going to sit outside in the pouring rain?

Now this may sound like a pretty feeble way to decorate a terrace, but let me tell you, the sight of all those gay pillows plopped around, plus the clay pots of inexpensive flowering plants (grown from seed), was a very pleasant one. We added a couple of small hibachis (those miniature Japanese hot-coal grills) and guests had a marvelous time sitting on the cushions and grilling their own tiny frankfurters or whatever on the hibachis. And as I pointed out to my client, when in the future the budget allowed for sofas and chairs, the pillows would go right on them, or provide extra seating for parties.

Here is another solution to the no-money-for-the-small-terrace problem. This tiny terrace was attached to a New York City apartment. We used deck chairs, those wonderful folding arm chairs with canvas seats and backs, comfortable and inexpensive, but not too exciting. We made them exciting by dyeing the white slip-off canvas seats and backs a sharp lemon-peel yellow. For tables we talked the local hardware store out of two nail kegs and sprayed them a glossy black. Big, plain glass plates (eighty cents each at the variety store) served as ashtrays; and pots of pink geraniums massed in a market basket gave just the right glow of color.

Sometimes very pretty garden furniture is to be found at thrift shops or "yard sales." I once did a terrace on a shoestring budget because I was lucky enough to find a very attractive table and six chairs (two arm and four straight) in very good quality wrought iron at a Salvation Army store. The problem was that it was sadly in need of paint and was quite rusty in spots. We first sprayed it with a coat of rust-proof base and then with a coat of sky blue enamel. Cushions were made for the chairs from blue and white bandanas (a dollar each at the variety store) and we planted two nail kegs, left in their natural wood state, with blue hydrangeas. Naturally we drilled holes in the bottoms and covered them with a layer of pebbles before adding the soil and the plants.

So far I've outlined a few things that can be done with very little money, but I'd like to caution you about a few things you don't need, no matter how little they cost. Please, I beg you, don't buy those ghastly plastic-strip pieces of outdoor furniture, particularly chairs and recliners of shiny metal with strips of plastic webbing forming the seats and backs. Sit on the ground first, buy a beach towel and lie on that, leave the terrace bare, if need be, but don't buy that horrible stuff—it is cheap-looking to the point of being hideous. Another thing you don't need is a huge, ungainly barbecue apparatus. If you have the money to have a simple brick grill built along a wall, fine; otherwise, settle for a hibachi or a simple foldaway grill that can be stored out of sight when not needed.

Also to be avoided at all or any cost are those awful stoneware ducks, geese and other assorted fauna found, usually, at roadside stands. Unless you have the money for really good garden ornaments, let them go in favor of clay pots filled with blooming plants or greenery.

The most absolutely hopeless outdoor job I ever tackled was a huge, barnlike deck outside an apartment for a girl who really didn't have any money at all to spend on it. It wasn't a matter of finding furniture for it at any price—there was no money to buy anything whatsoever. She had maybe fifty dollars to spare, and the deck was enormous. I finally decided to blow thirty-five of the fifty on a mammoth pine tree in a huge tub. (For some reason, pine trees, for all their great decorative value, are cheap. Don't ask me why, they just are.) We set the pine tree smack in the middle of the deck and, surprisingly, it immediately "furnished" that outdoor space! Then we managed to find a college boy who, for the fifteen dollars left, built a long, narrow bench against the railing for seating. My client is planning to add some plump cushions in colorful sailcloth (about two dollars per yard), as soon as the next paycheck arrives. However, in the meantime that deck doesn't look too bad. Once again it proves my theory that one big smashing thing is superior to a lot of inconsequential junk.

How can I tell you what to put on your particular porch, patio or terrace? I can only tell you to keep your eyes open. Should you stumble on a wonderful set of old wicker, by all means grab it if you can. Cover the seats with a lovely mélange of flowers or checked gingham, and add as many plants as you can acquire. This will really dress up a screened porch or flagstone terrace.

If you are in despair over a city terrace, try for one large tree or bush: pine, Japanese cherry or some other. Get a few captain's chairs, some nail kegs for tables, and let paint and dye be your decorating allies. Again, let honesty be your policy: real wood, stone, shells, sturdy cotton fabrics are best out-of-doors. Include among them real plants—flowering annuals and bulbs—and don't worry if things seem a little bare to start with. Reject the phony, the cheap, the obvious. Time is on your side. Give it a chance.

§§

CHAPTER TEN

ACCESSORIES--THAT PERFECT TOUCH

§§

ACCESSORIES can make or break a room. You can have the most harmonious color scheme, comfortable, attractive furniture and a pleasant arrangement, but add the wrong accessories and the whole thing is a mess. How to avoid it? Well, there are certain rules to the game that make it easier.

Lamps

First, let's take lamps. They are essential and utilitarian, of course, but they are also accessories. If there were no concern for esthetics, you could just switch on an overhead light. Until recently, about the only decent-looking lamp on the market at any price has been the Chinese ginger jar, or Chinese vase shape. Fortunately they are available in handsome colors, and the manufacturers have rediscovered the crisp, pleated paper shade. This combination can solve most of your lamp problems.

Gooseneck lamp.

A true thrift shop hound may just be able to pick up a real Chinese vase at a bargain and have it wired and mounted as a lamp. I once bought a blue-and-white Canton vase at an auction (in Del Ray, Florida, of all places), for $64. It's probably worth ten times that now, but I sold it for something in between, to a client who simply had to have it.

Aside from the Chinese jars or vases, I have grown to love the new, modern pole lamps with cylindrical shaded light. They seem to look so right in so many settings and have the happy habit of "disappearing." You have the light but are not aware of the lamp.

One perennially good lamp buy in thrift shops is the old-fashioned gooseneck office lamp, that old standby with a flat metal base and a flexible gooseneck stem. The light itself is shaded by a rounded metal shade and it has a marvelous "tacky chic" that's great on a desk or bedside table. Paint it if you like, though I prefer the worn look.

Ashtrays

Next on the list of essentials is ashtrays. Oh, how many sins are perpetrated in the design of same, but those gruesome objects shown in gift shops are not for us. Far more chic and far cheaper are pretty plates that are both functional and decorative. What kind? Well, usually the dessert-size plate is best. Look for English design, the Indian tree pattern, for example. This is the Indian Tree of Life in dark crimson on a cream-colored background. Or the Blind Earl pattern, so-called because it was created for the blind Duke of Northumberland. Or anything Chinese . . . for some reason Chinese accent pieces seem to go with any décor, even Early American—after all, the clipper ships returned to New England well loaded with "Canton ware." Even the 18th-century French admired "Chinoiserie" and used Chinese accents with Louis XV or XVI furniture.

By Chinese I don't mean those dreadful imitation Oriental dishes heavily loaded with gilt and sold as "decorative" plates. Don't buy anything, for that matter, that is called "decorative" or "decorator-styled." Try to find plates and cups and saucers that were once part of a dinner service; as odd pieces they are not too expensive and can be lovely. I like to use the plates as generous-sized ashtrays, and cups and saucers to hold cigarettes and matches. Matches! That brings me to a point that though small can be most important. Never, no never, allow those folders of paper matches that bear a legend such as "Draw Me" or "Free Shoes" or some other advertisement in your house. Plain kitchen matches are okay, even those little boxes of safety matches aren't hideous. If you like and can afford them, match folders in pretty colors are available. Please, though, no initials, or labels like "Bob and Mary" or "Our Place." Unless you live on an estate and the estate has a name, leave your match folders anonymous, please.

Cigarette Boxes

Now for cigarette boxes. In general the boxes that are manufactured to hold cigarettes are pretty grim unless you have the money to buy Baccarat crystal ones. But that's not very thrifty. Unless you find a wonderful old tin box, or some other fascinating small box, I'd say skip covered containers and put cigarettes out in interesting old cups, or in small baskets.

I found a wonderful old crystal inkwell minus its top that holds seven or eight cigarettes and looks great on my desk.

Pictures

Pictures and other wall decorations are next on the accessory list, and frankly, they are the biggest traps of all. The first rule to follow: *Don't be afraid of bare walls*. Quite honestly, unless you are very discerning you should stay away from original paintings. Real talent is quickly recognized, and just as quickly becomes high-priced. Unless you are both knowledgeable and lucky, the chances of "discovering" a really good artist are slim. Groups of prints can be attractive over a table or desk, but again, move with caution. I once found a pair of English boxing prints that looked great in the hallway, but I am the first to admit that this was pure luck. As for the usual trite sets of English coaching scenes or vapid flower prints, you are better off with nothing on the wall. You can get by with just a handsome big mirror, good-looking lamps to give height, and a couple of big dried-flower arrangements.

For example, I recently did over a small apartment for a couple with more taste than money. The walls we painted the color of bamboo, the sofa and chairs we covered in beige duck, the wall opposite was mirrored and centered with an old "hall" table freshly lacquered dark blue. We hung a large mirror over the sofa and placed a substantial-size ginger-jar lamp in dark blue with a pleated white shade at one end of the table. The opposite end of the table held a basket of dried field flowers and everything reflected back and forth. Since one of the other walls was a pair of glass doors leading to a small planted terrace the fourth wall was centered by a right-angled desk-table arrangement with its own good-looking lamp. Wall pictures were not missed at all.

Some other things to avoid putting on your walls are those awful pressed-wood mirrors and candelabra. No, a thousand times no. In fact, it's far better to avoid anything that's made to look like something else, or a copy of something. Have the real thing, whatever it is, great or small, lavish or modest.

Floors

From walls to floors is not a false move, for though you can hardly call a floor an accessory, what you put on it, in a strange way, is. The reason for this is that most people regard a floor simply as a floor; it is either wood or carpeted or covered with vinyl, and that's it. Not so at all. Floors can be the most decorative asset you can have. It's how you handle them that makes the difference.

First of all, I hope you don't have wall-to-wall carpeting and, if you don't, that you won't buy it. If you are stuck, as I have sometimes been, with a so-called "luxury" apartment that's been carpeted throughout (not for the sake of luxury but actually to save money for the builder), then you'll simply have to cope with it—and move out as soon as you can.

Wall-to-wall carpeting is dull, dreary, and dirty. I hate the stuff so much that I once persuaded an apartment landlord to let me take it back up and replace it with a good-looking vinyl floor of black-and-white sixteen by sixteen-inch tiles laid in a diamond pattern. All at my expense, needless to say. Expensive, but I just couldn't stand that carpeting.

If you are fortunate enough to have good or even handsome

Oriental rug.

Grass rug.

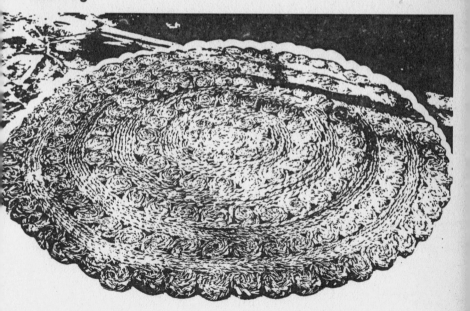

wood floors, then all you have to do is stain them as dark as possible, wax and buff them. Paste wax, please—you simply cannot get the same soft gleam with liquid wax, I don't care what it says on the can. With beautiful wood floors, you want as little rug as possible, perhaps a needlepoint that you have made yourself placed in front of the sofa, a soft, faded Oriental, or, if you really want to save money, try one of those interesting raffia rugs in its own natural colors. A good size costs about thirty dollars, a lot of decorating for the money.

But what if the floors are terrible wood, or worse yet, concrete? (The builder was counting on your buying wall-to-wall.) Then the only thing to do is turn to paint and vinyl. If the really bad floors are wood and can be sanded smooth, they can be painted and should be done in a dark color: deep maroon (almost a black); dark, dark blue; black brown; or true black. You are going to need at least two coats of floor and deck paint, and a liquid vinyl sealer. Painted floors hold up better than you would think, if carefully done, each coat allowed to dry completely before the next is applied. Once the floor is completely dry it can be kept looking very respectable with a vinyl-type liquid wax. If you have a reliable paint store in your town, consult the manager on what paint to use for your particular floors; if not, write for information to Janovic Plaza Paints (see page 55).

For covering concrete floors, vinyl tile is perhaps the best answer—you can get marvelous effects with it. I like best the diamond pattern in black and white, or the hexagon-shaped Spanish tile in deep clay color. Both have the classic good looks of marble or tile and either one goes with any décor except true Early American. If that's your atmosphere you'll have to settle for a brick effect, which isn't bad. (Actually I don't think any room should be exclusively true early anything—it's far too limiting.)

Let's see, we've covered lamps, ashtrays, cigarette boxes, walls and floors. Now for the extra accessory, or what I call the little extras that bring a room to life. High on my list are candlesticks, brass ones, particularly; I like to collect singles, which are cheaper than pairs. I especially like to use a tall one covered by a glass hurricane shade. This arrangement is a lot of decoration for the money, and even more so if it is placed in front of a mirror. Try placing candles around a room, on a coffee table, a dressing table, in a hall; they really add sparkle and life to any room. I have candles in holders in my kitchen, and once I even had a kitchen party illuminated only by candles.

As for pitchers and bowls for flowers, why not buy yourself an heirloom? Your selection of china might include such pieces. Currently the Historic Charleston Foundation is sponsoring reproductions of the antiques of that lovely old rose-brick city, and one of the most outstanding is perfectly authentic copies of Canton ware. Not only are the serving plates and cups and saucers perfectly beautiful, and a delight to use, but the coffee service and pitchers and bowls are perfect accent display pieces. I use the tall milk pitchers for fall flowers, the cream pitcher for small bouquets. The coffee service sits on a side table in the dining room. Like most Chinese classics, Canton ware, even in reproduction, "goes" with almost any style of room. The prices are hardly thrift shop, but if you can swing it, you'll get your money's worth over the years. The same holds true for most classic Chinese patterns, but I have to admit that Canton is outstanding. Write to Mottahedeh (see page 70) or directly to Historic Charleston Reproductions, King at Broad Street, Charleston, South Carolina 29401.

Other heirlooms you might find include lovely old boxes of tin, wood or lacquer. I have an old red lacquer Chinese box that I literally carried around the world with me during my stint as a Navy officer's wife. Now, twenty years later, it sits serenely on my desk, safe, and glowing at me, a joy every time I see it. And that's what an accessory should be—a thing of beauty and joy forever. Don't try to accessorize your room all at once; wait until the right thing comes along, as it most certainly will. The marvelous big basket to hold magazines, the old painted wooden figurine for a side table, the perfect thing that you *must* have—that's the way to select the "extra accessory."

§§

CHAPTER ELEVEN

DECORATING WITH PLANTS AND FLOWERS

§§

ONE of the easiest ways I know for the thrift shop decorator to give a room the look of luxury at little cost is to learn how to use plants and flowers. You can actually add a "piece of furniture" with a big armload of green leaves arranged in a sizable container. Surprisingly enough, a graceful tree or a tray of flourishing fern set on a polished floor immediately cures the barren look. By the time you can afford the rug you want, you may find the indoor greenery so effective you won't want the rug at all. But there's more to decorating with plants than sticking a pot of philodendrons on the mantelpiece. (In fact, no philodendrons at all, please.)

The first rule of decorating with plants and flowers is that they must look luxuriant and healthy. Better a mass of paper zinnias than three not-so-hot roses, or a big pot of flourishing ferns rather than a sickly palm tree. Plants should be alive and vigorous, and they will be with just a little care. Flower arrangements should show imagination and make a definite statement, a real contribution to the room as a whole.

Let's deal first with plants; the absolute essential for healthy plants is light and plenty of it. No green plant will grow without an abundance of light, and few, if any, will flower without sunlight. If you are so unfortunate, as I have been at times, in having to put up with a dark apartment, there's no point in wasting money on plants; concentrate on long-lived flower arrangements and leaves instead (more on this later). But never, no never, substitute plastic plants for the real thing. The whole point of plants is to have growing greens in your house, and a dusty fake plant is an insult to the eye.

Now with that little lecture behind us, let's go on to the happier assumption that you have loads of light and perhaps even some direct sunlight, and that you are also willing to invest a little time in caring for your plants. If so, you can have a marvelous time adding to your rooms finishing touches in the form of green growing things.

Let's begin with the living room. In my opinion, the most decorative plant of all is a ficus tree. In case you are not familiar with a ficus, it is a graceful, tall plant with a gray-brown bark and glossy green oval-shaped leaves. It is usually umbrella shaped, that is, a tall narrow trunk topped with a downward-curving abundance of leaves. It is extremely graceful and never fails to add interest and drama to any room. Ficus trees do have some drawbacks, however—for one, they are a bit expensive (anywhere from fifty to one hundred dollars, depending on size and where you buy them), a very good reason to avoid them unless you have plenty of money and are willing to give them the growing conditions they need. They must have moisture—a too dry, overheated room is sure death—and they

Boston fern in a hanging basket.

must have an abundance of light. If you can meet these conditions you will be rewarded by more decorative value than you can get from any other plant. And, dollar for dollar, more decoration than from any other single thing you can add to your room. Basic care is the same as for most plants: water sparingly, test the soil with your fingers and if it is reasonably damp, hold off on the water. The soil should never be actually dry, but overwatering is the most common cause of failure in house plants. All plants should be fertilized every six weeks to two months. I like fish-emulsion fertilizer best. It's simple to use—just follow the directions on the bottle; and it's available in just about any plant or seed shop. I must warn you it smells horrible, but the odor quickly vanishes so don't be alarmed. (I only hope you won't run into the unusual problem it created for me. For some unknown reason my wire-haired terrier regarded it as nectar of the gods and would try madly to eat the soil out of the pots after the fish-emulsion treatment. I still don't know why.)

Where should you put a tree? As mentioned before, where it will get as much light as possible; after that spot is found, you can go on from there. A tall tree looks very handsome next to a fairly big table or behind a sofa; in fact it's hard to place a good tree badly since it is such effective decoration.

Next on my list of favorite plants are Boston ferns. They are easy to grow and give a marvelous effect if they are big enough—and *big* they should be. better one huge fern than ten dinky ones. Boston ferns are not terribly expensive either and flatter almost any room. Whatever you do, insist on buying your ferns in clay pots. Plastic pots are hideous, and worse yet, plants do not do as well in them—they need the porous clay to breathe. Ferns in clay pots look fine just about anywhere, in bedrooms and bathrooms as well as living and dining rooms. To my mind they look best grouped on a pebble-filled tray on the floor. Or a single fern can be placed in a handsome old basket on a table, or on the floor in a small hallway.

Palm trees can be effective, too, but frankly they have been used so much I'm a little tired of them. If you don't share my ennui with the palm tree there's no reason why you can't have one wherever you like. I think they look best growing in big baskets, but I once placed one in a nice old brass coal scuttle in a very traditional living room in Charleston, South Carolina, and it was very handsome.

Surprisingly enough, orchids are not difficult to grow. Try them. Again we are dealing with a tropical plant, and like the ficus and the palm, orchids require ample light and moisture. They are easy enough to care for if you devote a little attention to them. The initial cost of an orchid can be a little steep, but given reasonable care it will reward you with an abundance of decoration for the money. I'm talking about the little brown or yellow orchids, not the big, showy purple ones—those we will reserve for some unfortunate mother of the bride. But the delicate little spray orchids are heaven in almost any room setting.

As for other flowering plants, I'll be honest: about the only ones I have successfully grown indoors are African violets. I happen to love geraniums, but every time I've tried growing them indoors the poor things have collapsed; they simply must have full sunlight, at least *mine* do. African violets, on the other hand, seem to flourish if placed on a tray of pebbles and watered by pouring a scant amount of water into the tray whenever they seem at all dry. Some sunlight is required, and above all, never leave them in a dry, overheated atmosphere, or they will die.

If you are serious about growing plants indoors (and you had better be if you try at all—they aren't cheap), spend a few dollars for a plastic mist sprayer and spray your plants with a fine mist every few days. These are available at almost any variety store or flower shop and are well worth the little they cost. It's the closest you can come to treating your plants to natural rainfall.

A more luxurious substitute (if you can afford it—I never can) is to buy an electric room humidifier. This device automatically keeps the air just moist enough to make plants and complexions flourish. It's wonderful for steam-heated houses and apartments, and it gives the added bonus of saving your furniture from drying and cracking. I've always wanted one or two.

Naturally there are any number of other plants you can grow indoors. I have only touched on the subject; you and a good plant catalogue can probably come up with dozens more. The important thing is to consider the decorative effect they will have in your rooms. Basically, plants should make an emphatic statement; pallid little pots of plants from the dime store are worse than no plants at all. To be avoided at all costs are those miniature gardens. Whether Japanese, Mexican or Hindu does not matter in the least, they are all awful—don't let anybody talk you into one. Your best bet in buying plants is a reliable florist or greenhouse; try to find one who seems interested and who really loves plants. Those florists whose shops are filled with plastic flowers and "canned" arrangements that tie in with Mother's Day, Easter, Thanksgiving, etc., are the ones to stay clear of. If their advertising stresses funeral or wedding arrangements, run fast in the opposite direction.

Back to the less fortunate souls whose rooms are not flooded with light. You need not give up plants and greenery, nor do you have to spend a fortune on fresh flowers. If you are really short of cash (and how well I know that situation), you can get marvelous effects with big bouquets of green leaves that usually sell for around a dollar a bunch. Ask for rhododendron or magnolia or lemon leaves, or a combination of two, and plan to arrange them in a big basket that will hold a deep pot of water. Or if you have any handsome large container such as the brass coal scuttle mentioned earlier, use that instead. Even if you don't own such a container, you can still have your greenery. Get a small washtub for a few dollars and spray-paint it shiny black. You'll be amazed how handsome it looks filled with glossy green leaves. Finally, another nice thing about leaves is that they last for weeks if you give them fresh water every five or six days.

As for flowers, I'll admit that unless you have a greenhouse, cut flowers run into money. But if you stick to seasonal blooms they are not prohibitive. Zinnias happen to be a favorite of mine; their wonderful showy colors look great almost anywhere, and they last for at least a week. Again, like most flowers, they look best in baskets. Let me digress to containers for cut flowers, for a moment. Those wretched things the lady from Lower Slobovia refers to as "va-a-ses" should never enter your house. If you own any, throw them out, give them away or donate them to a charity thrift shop. I don't care if they are antique blown glass that your mother and father brought back from Bavaria on the Queen Elizabeth, get rid of them, the sooner the better. Flowers belong in simple, honest things like baskets, nice clean-lined pitchers, old milk cans, copper and silver bowls. Small arrangements look best in plain mugs or wine glasses. Anything decorated or "fancied up" is to be avoided at all costs.

So much for that long-winded lecture on containers; let's get back to flowers. Daisies are another long-lasting cut flower that is usually quite reasonable, especially if you live where you can buy them at a local flower or fruit and vegetable stand.

Flower people are usually wonderful people to deal with; some of the most pleasant experiences of my life have centered around flower dealers. There is the wonderful and knowledgeable Mr. Koster of the elegant and lush Christatos and Koster (709 Madison Avenue, New York, New York 10021). Mr. Koster always had time to help me find a bargain and to give valuable free advice on plants and long-lasting blooms. Then, far away in Charleston, South Carolina, there were the flower ladies who sold their wares on the street in front of the post office across from the venerable St. Michael's Church. My favorite was Annabelle, whose intelligent face always broke into a smile when she saw me. From the daffodils in January to the Christmas greens in December, I never made a trip to the post office and came home empty handed. In Southampton, Long Island, there is the wonderful Mrs. Knight, who not only has "just-picked-this-morning" fruits and vegetables, but masses of summer flowers at reasonable prices. All too often at her stand I forget the fresh corn and tomatoes for dinner in favor of an armload of snapdragons, zinnias, marigolds and daisies. (Knight's Farms, North Main Street, Southampton, New York 11968.)

When the summer bounty of flowers is at its height, have you thought of wild flowers? Not too many keep well after cutting (and please do cut carefully and prudently), but I have had great luck with wild daisies and Queen Anne's lace, and so may you. And no one can quarrel with the price.

But what about the winter months when flowers are rare and

expensive? Well, I like then to buy a couple of pots of chrysan-themums. Kept well watered, they will stay blooming for at least a couple of weeks. When November rolls around I always ask my florist for a few Stars of Bethlehem; these lovely, big white flowers last literally for weeks. They cost a bit to start with, but they are so spectacular that three or four make a good showing.

Once Christmas is upon us, I always find time to plant a few paperwhite narcissus in pebble-filled containers. They usually flower in a few weeks, given any light at all, and they see me through till spring flowers are with us again.

Failing anything else, there are all sorts of dried grasses that make wonderful long-lasting arrangements. The one artificial flower I like is the wonderful paper zinnias mentioned before.

The important thing is to let flowers and plants add life to your rooms; a house without something green or flowering is indeed barren and lifeless. Decorating does not mean building a mausoleum or museum, but creating a pleasant ambience in which to live.

§§

CHAPTER TWELVE

SOME RANDOM THOUGHTS

§§§

NO room should be all "brand new"; it will lack a human quality.

I wish people wouldn't worry so much about matching colors; if you stay with natural color combinations, variations can only be improvements on a theme.

Furniture arrangements should be logical and they should work. If they don't the room is badly done and a total loss.

Entranceways speak loudly; the most beautiful house or apartment is wasted if the front door is not inviting and the hall or entranceway fresh and attractive.

Furniture advertisers (with a few notable exceptions) are completely lacking in even the bare fundamentals of taste. Don't listen to them.

Avoid furniture stores the way you would Typhoid Mary. They are almost always filled with gaudy junk at fantastically inflated prices.

Never buy furniture on a time-payment plan. Not only will you overpay for the most horrible objects, but you will pay eighteen to twenty-four percent interest besides. Get by with thrift shop pieces until you can afford a fine antique or a great modern piece available only through a decorator.

Did you know that nearly any decorator will purchase furniture, as well as other furnishings, for you? He or she makes thirty percent on the deal, but you get the particular piece you want.

Lighting can be a great asset or a disaster. The most common fault is too much light. Never use a seventy-five or one hundred watt bulb in anything but a kitchen fixture. Even bathrooms do better with two sixty-watt bulbs rather than one hundred watt. Light should flow gently in a room, not overwhelm it. Try using more lamps and lower-watt bulbs, either frosted or tinted, for maximum good looks.

I wonder why more people don't learn to make needlepoint rugs. They are actually fun to work, and nothing adds more character to a room than a rug you have made yourself.

Isn't it annoying that some people insist that only a house can be a home? Does this mean an apartment is not a home? You can go home or come home, but you cannot buy or rent a home. You can buy or rent a house and make it your home, or you can make an apartment into your home. You have to transform one into the other and that's what decorating is all about.

"Likewise, I'm sure," said the lady from Lower Slobovia, who then invited the assembled company to see her beautiful home and gorgeous "drapes." Was she planning some sort of Roman entertainment, with the players draped in togas? Or could she have been referring to her curtains? You can drape a figure, or a table, but those things at the window are curtains, no matter what they cost or how elaborate they are. They may be topped by a valance, or what the British call a pelmet (a fabric-covered wooden frame), or they may be simple organdy, but they still remain curtains, and the drapes stay on the Roman actors.

Imagination and a sense of the good life are essential to successful decorating—at any price. The imaginative person visualizes how the room is to be used. For example, imagine yourself entertaining at a very British afternoon tea. Right away your mind conjures up a room of soft flower colors, a blazing fire behind gleaming brass andirons, the whole thing softly illuminated against the chill of a winter afternoon. Or imagine a porch party on a summer evening, the wicker and rattan furniture grouped around the potted trees and plants, the light coming softly from Japanese lanterns attached to ceiling fixtures and illuminated with small, low-watt bulbs.

Or it's Christmas and your dining table is set for a festive meal. The walls are deep crimson, the curtains and chair seats are red and pink roses on white chintz. The table is set with crimson cotton mats and napkins, and the centerpiece is some sort of sparkly crystal, perhaps a collection of crystal animals. Do you see what I mean? Let your imagination do your decorating. It really works.

Don't be afraid of color, the decorating magazines say. That's very inspiring, but it's a good idea to have a little fear before you get in so deep you can't get out. I know a young couple with very daring ideas who painted one wall of each room a different color from the remaining three. It was certainly colorful, but it was also chaotic. Six months went by before the couple could afford to repaint those odd walls to match their neighbors'. A rather costly bit of daring, wouldn't you say?

Never *try* to be "elegant." If your decorating is honest, with good color, a logical arrangement of furniture and a fresh, orderly look, it will *be* elegant. You won't succeed with fussy fabrics, elaborate extra accessories and aiming for the so-called "rich" look. Remember, less is always more.

How I hate venetian blinds. Noisy, dirty, expensive and ordinary looking—a pox on them! Curtains that pull together at night or bamboo shades that roll up easily are a thousand times better, and cost far less. *Right!*

You have to have a deep sense of home to decorate well. If your decorating attempt is a means of showing off to your friends, or of providing a background for parties, it will never come off. Successful decorating means allowing for children and pets, for the cooking of memorable meals, for spending happy times alone. In essence, creating a haven from the pressures of the outside world. The stiff, coordinated room where no one moves an ashtray is not decorated, it is embalmed.

All the furniture, fabrics, colors and accessories are meaningless without a large dose of tender loving care. The brass must shine, the flowers must be fresh, the furniture must be waxed and polished. The fire should be built, the plants tended, and the washables frequently laundered. All these things are work but it's a labor of love without which you may as well move to a furnished room.

The well-decorated house has a well-decorated refrigerator, pantry and bar. What's the point of the inviting living room or the charming dining room if you cannot ask a friend in for a drink or a meal on the spur of the moment? There should be a tray for cocktails in the living room and a good-looking ice bucket ready to be filled at a moment's notice. Stock quick-to-assemble meals in the refrigerator or pantry.

Good decorating at any price is attention to details, matches in the match boxes, cigarettes in theirs, pillows plumped to perfection, a tiny bouquet on a bathroom counter, interesting reading in a basket.

Why don't you buy one real lead crystal whiskey-sour glass and use it for cigarettes on your coffee table? Lead crystal is expensive but one glass won't set you back that much. You can serve drinks in any plain glass from the dime store and no one is going to notice. Meanwhile the sparkling beauty on the coffee table is there for all to observe—an effective touch.

A dozen red-and-white or blue-and-white cotton bandanas (about a dollar each) can be used as napkins for a buffet table. Combine them with inexpensive glass plates and a centerpiece of red geraniums in clay pots, or a bowl of polished red apples, depending on the season.

Plan to have a centerpiece of real lemons and fresh green lemon leaves for your next dinner party.

Skip a centerpiece completely at the dinner party after that. Instead, have a tiny pot of real herbs at each guest's place. (Let your guests take them home as lasting favors.)

Have you ever thought of renting a painting from your local museum? It usually costs only a few dollars a month, and the rental is almost always applied to the purchase price if you fall in love with the painting and want it permanently.

Lacquer an old tin tray (almost always available at thrift shops) in a lovely color—Chinese red, lemon-peel yellow, olive-green, dark blue. Place it on an inexpensive luggage rack for an effective and handy coffee table.

Pick up some old damask napkins at an auction (or thrift shop) and dye them a pale ecru beige if they have coffee stains. They would be lovely with a centerpiece of dried grasses or shells.

Use a pretty saucer or dish to hold soap in your bathroom or powder room. Much more attractive than a prosaic standard soap dish.

Arrange a few bare branches in a Chinese ginger jar or a pretty pitcher. Place it where the branches are silhouetted against a blank wall when the lights are turned on.

Invest a few dollars in some marvelous foreign magazines on decoration and pile them on your coffee table. Attractive, interesting and informative.

Check the yellow pages of your telephone book for chemist's supplies and buy a few clear glass chemist's beakers for flowers, or for oil and vinegar. Inexpensive and effective.

Buy a few tiny baskets at the variety store and use them for matches.

Want to make your house smell as nice as it looks? Try drying any flowers that come your way. Spread them out on newspapers in a dry place—roses work especially well. Then pile them in a pretty bowl, add a few drops of rose or jasmine oil, and there you are with your own potpourri.

Or make some fragrant pomander balls to hang in your closets. These are oranges stuck all over with cloves and allowed to dry. Tie with velvet ribbon and attach to coat hangers. You can intensify the fragrance with pomander oil if you like.

Ingredients for both potpourri and pomander balls can be ordered from the catalog of Caswell-Massey, Inc., 320 West 13th Street, New York, New York 10014.

Resolve to use your ingenuity to have the most charming house in town.